AF693464

MASTERING THE SERIES 7 EXAM

MASTERING THE SERIES 7 EXAM

THE ULTIMATE GUIDE TO BECOMING A LICENSED SECURITIES REPRESENTATIVE

Written By

D.W. LINDSEY

Mastering The Series - 7 Exam
D.W. Lindsey

All rights reserved
First Edition, 2025
© D.W. Lindsey, 2025

No part of this publication may be reproduced, or stored in a retrieval system, or transmitted in any form by means of electronic, mechanical, photocopying or otherwise, without prior written permission from the author.

Flames Creations | Design Services Provided by Flames Creations

TABLE OF CONTENTS

INTRODUCTION

The financial industry is a competitive and fast-paced field that requires professionals to have a deep understanding of investment products, regulations, and ethical standards. One of the most important steps in becoming a securities representative is passing the Series 7 Exam, a comprehensive test that evaluates a candidate's knowledge of financial markets, investment strategies, and compliance regulations. This exam is not just another certification—it is a gateway to a rewarding career in the securities industry.

In this book, we will explore everything you need to know about the Series 7 Exam, why it matters, and how this guide will help you succeed.s

OVERVIEW OF THE SERIES 7 EXAM

The Series 7 Exam, officially known as the General Securities Representative Exam (GSRE), is administered by the Financial Industry Regulatory Authority (FINRA).

It is designed to test the knowledge and competency of individuals who want to become registered representatives and work in the securities industry. Passing this exam allows financial professionals to buy and sell securities such as stocks, bonds, mutual funds, and options on behalf of clients.

The exam is known for its broad scope, covering topics such as:

- Types of securities and financial instruments
- Investment risks and strategies
- Regulatory requirements and ethical responsibilities
- Customer interactions and recommendations
- Trading and execution of orders

The Series 7 Exam consists of 125 multiple-choice questions, and candidates are given 225 minutes (3 hours and 45 minutes) to complete it. To pass, you must score at least 72%. While the exam is challenging, a well-structured study plan and the right resources can make the process much easier.

Before taking the Series 7 Exam, candidates must first pass the Securities Industry Essentials (SIE) Exam and be sponsored by a FINRA-member firm. The SIE Exam covers basic concepts related to financial markets and securities regulations, serving as an entry-level test for those interested in the industry.

WHY THE SERIES 7 EXAM IS IMPORTANT FOR FINANCIAL PROFESSIONALS

If you're serious about building a career in the financial services industry, passing the Series 7 Exam is a major milestone. It is one of the most widely recognized securities licensing exams and provides professionals with the necessary credentials to work as a registered representative. Here's why this exam is so important:

- Without passing the Series 7 Exam, you cannot legally sell securities such as stocks, bonds, and mutual funds. Many firms require their employees to hold this license before they can advise clients or execute trades. In short, this exam is your entry ticket to becoming a financial professional.

- Having a Series 7 license significantly improves your career prospects. It makes you more valuable to employers, increases your credibility with clients, and allows you to explore different roles within the financial industry. Many professionals who start as registered representatives eventually move into roles such as financial advisors, investment analysts, and portfolio managers.

- The financial industry is built on trust. Clients want to work with professionals who are knowledgeable, ethical, and qualified to handle their investments. Passing the Series 7 Exam shows that you have the expertise to guide clients through complex financial decisions while following industry regulations.

- Many professionals use the Series 7 license as a stepping stone for advanced certifications such as the Chartered Financial Analyst (CFA) designation, the Certified Financial Planner (CFP) certification, or the Series 66 license (which allows representatives to act as investment advisors).

- The Series 7 Exam does not just test your knowledge of investments—it also ensures that you understand the laws and regulations governing the securities industry. Compliance is a critical aspect of the financial sector, and professionals who fail to follow industry rules can face serious penalties, including fines or suspension.

Let's get started on your journey to mastering the Series 7 Exam!

PART 1:

UNDERSTANDING THE SERIES 7 EXAM

CHAPTER 1
EXAM BASICS

WHO NEEDS THE SERIES 7 LICENSE?

The Series 7 license is one of the most recognized certifications in the financial industry, especially for those looking to build a career in securities trading. It is required for individuals who want to engage in the buying and selling of financial instruments such as stocks, bonds, mutual funds, and options. This license is widely used in brokerage firms, investment banks, and other financial institutions that deal with securities transactions.

Professionals who obtain the Series 7 license gain the ability to execute trades and offer investment advice, making them valuable assets in the finance industry. Since securities trading involves handling client investments and following strict regulations, it is necessary for professionals to be properly licensed to ensure compliance with industry rules.

Stockbrokers and Registered Representatives

Stockbrokers, also known as registered representatives, need the Series 7 license to buy and sell securities on behalf of clients. These professionals work for brokerage firms and help investors build and manage their portfolios. A stockbroker's role goes beyond simply executing trades—they must also understand the financial goals of their clients, provide investment advice, and ensure that transactions are in line with industry regulations.

Registered representatives are expected to analyze market trends, recommend suitable investments, and follow ethical guidelines when dealing with client accounts. The Series 7 license grants them the legal authority to perform these tasks, ensuring that they operate within the framework of securities laws and regulations.

Financial Advisors

Many financial advisors choose to obtain the Series 7 license to expand the range of services they can provide to their clients. Without this license, their ability to recommend and sell certain types of securities is limited. Having the Series 7 license allows financial advisors to offer a more comprehensive investment strategy to their clients, including diversified portfolios that include stocks, bonds, options, and mutual funds.

Financial advisors play a key role in guiding clients toward their financial goals. They assess a client's financial situation, risk tolerance, and long-term objectives before making investment recommendations. Since investment planning involves a variety of financial products, having the Series 7 license helps advisors give clients access to a wider selection of investment opportunities.

Investment Bankers

Investment bankers working in firms that deal with securities often need the Series 7 license, especially if their role involves selling securities or advising clients on investment strategies. While investment bankers primarily focus on mergers, acquisitions, and capital raising, those involved in selling financial instruments or dealing with institutional investors may need this license to ensure they operate within the legal framework of the industry.

For investment bankers, the Series 7 license enhances credibility and demonstrates their ability to handle securities transactions professionally. Since investment banking requires strong knowledge of market regulations and financial products, obtaining this license provides an added advantage in terms of career growth and professional recognition.

Portfolio Managers

While not always mandatory, some portfolio managers choose to obtain the Series 7 license to deepen their understanding of securities trading. A portfolio manager's primary responsibility is to oversee investment funds and manage assets on behalf of clients, institutions, or investment firms. Having a Series 7 license allows them to execute trades more efficiently and enhances their knowledge of market regulations.

Portfolio managers analyze market conditions, assess risk factors, and make investment decisions based on client objectives. Since they work with a wide range of investment products, having a strong foundation in securities trading can be beneficial for their role. The Series 7 license helps portfolio managers stay updated on compliance requirements and industry standards.

Wealth Managers

Wealth managers handle investment strategies for high-net-worth individuals and institutional clients. They develop long-term investment plans, manage portfolios, and provide personalized financial advice. The Series 7 license enables wealth managers to offer a complete range of investment products, ensuring that their clients have access to a diversified portfolio.

For wealth managers, having the Series 7 license is a significant advantage because it allows them to tailor investment strategies based on market conditions and client needs. It also ensures that they are well-versed in compliance rules and ethical responsibilities when handling client accounts.

Traders

Individuals who trade securities for investment firms, hedge funds, or proprietary trading firms often need the Series 7 license. Traders execute buy and sell orders based on market trends and client instructions. Since securities trading requires a thorough understanding of financial instruments, having the Series 7 license ensures that traders operate within legal and ethical boundaries.

Professional traders must analyze market data, develop trading strategies, and respond quickly to price movements. The Series 7 license provides them with the regulatory knowledge required to execute trades effectively and avoid compliance violations.

Financial Consultants

Some financial consultants obtain the Series 7 license to provide more specialized investment advice to their clients. Financial consultants may work independently or as part of advisory firms, helping individuals and businesses develop financial plans and investment strategies. Having the Series 7 license allows them to offer investment products and provide deeper insights into securities trading.

Consultants with a Series 7 license have a competitive advantage in the financial industry, as they can offer a broader range of services compared to those without it. This certification enhances their ability to recommend investment opportunities and align strategies with client goals.

WHO DOES NOT NEED THE SERIES 7 LICENSE?

Not all financial professionals require a Series 7 license. Some roles in the finance industry focus more on financial planning, tax advising, or accounting, which do not involve securities trading.

For example, financial planners who only provide advice without executing trades do not need the Series 7 license. Instead, they might pursue certifications such as the Certified Financial Planner (CFP) designation, which focuses on holistic financial planning rather than securities transactions.

Similarly, accountants and tax advisors who assist clients with financial planning but do not engage in securities trading do not need this license. Their expertise lies in tax strategies, compliance, and financial reporting rather than investment management.

Professionals involved in real estate investments also do not require a Series 7 license unless they are dealing with securities related to Real Estate Investment Trusts (REITs) or other financial instruments tied to real estate.

Before taking the Series 7 Exam, candidates must pass the Securities Industry Essentials (SIE) Exam and be sponsored by a FINRA-member firm. Sponsorship ensures that candidates are affiliated with a financial institution that oversees their professional activities and compliance responsibilities.

EXAM STRUCTURE AND FORMAT

The Series 7 Exam is designed to test a candidate's knowledge of securities trading, financial regulations, investment strategies, and ethical considerations. It is a multiple-choice exam that evaluates how well a candidate understands the responsibilities of a registered securities representative.

The exam consists of 125 multiple-choice questions, with a total time limit of 225 minutes (3 hours and 45 minutes). The minimum passing score is 72%, which means candidates must answer at least 90 questions correctly to pass.

In addition to the scored questions, the exam may include experimental questions that are used to test new question formats for future exams. These questions do not affect a candidate's score, but they are not identified separately from the scored questions.

The Series 7 Exam is structured into four major sections, each covering a different aspect of securities trading and customer interactions. These sections focus on:

- Seeking business from customers and potential customers
- Evaluating customers' financial situations and making suitable investment recommendations
- Providing customers with information about investments, executing trades, and maintaining proper records
- Verifying purchase and sales instructions, executing transactions, and ensuring regulatory compliance

Each section is designed to assess a candidate's ability to apply securities knowledge in real-world scenarios. The questions require candidates to understand market regulations, assess risk factors, and follow ethical guidelines when dealing with client accounts.

The exam is conducted electronically, and candidates receive their results immediately after completing the test. If a candidate does not pass, they must wait 30 days before retaking the exam. If they fail three times, they must wait six months before attempting it again.

The Series 7 Exam is a crucial step for professionals looking to enter the securities industry. It ensures that individuals handling securities transactions are well-trained, knowledgeable, and capable of following industry regulations. With proper preparation and study strategies, candidates can successfully pass the exam and obtain their Series 7 license, opening the door to a rewarding career in finance.

KEY TOPICS COVERED

The Series 7 Exam is designed to assess the knowledge and competency of candidates who wish to work as registered securities representatives. The exam tests a broad range of topics that are essential for professionals in the securities industry. Understanding these key topics is crucial for success in the exam and for future career growth.

The exam content is structured to cover four primary areas that mirror the responsibilities of a general securities representative. These areas include customer interactions, investment product knowledge, trade execution, and regulatory compliance. Each of these sections requires a deep understanding of securities markets, investment risks, legal responsibilities, and ethical considerations.

1. Seeking Business from Customers and Potential Customers

This section evaluates a candidate's ability to build client relationships and solicit business while adhering to industry regulations. It accounts for 9% of the exam and covers fundamental topics related to prospecting clients, ethical communication, and ensuring compliance in marketing activities.

Candidates must understand the different types of clients they may work with, including individual investors, institutional clients, and business entities. The ability to assess the financial needs of these clients is critical for making appropriate investment recommendations.

Additionally, this section emphasizes rules related to cold calling, marketing, and advertising. The Telephone Consumer Protection Act (TCPA) sets restrictions on how securities representatives can reach out to potential clients. Violating these rules can result in penalties, making it important for candidates to understand the legal requirements for soliciting business.

This section also highlights ethical considerations, such as ensuring that marketing materials are not misleading and that potential clients are given accurate information about investment opportunities. Securities professionals must operate with integrity, ensuring that they do not make false promises or misrepresent investment risks.

2. Evaluating Customers' Investment Profiles and Recommending Suitable Investment Products

This section, which accounts for 14% of the exam, focuses on assessing a client's financial situation and recommending investment products that align with their goals. It requires a thorough understanding of suitability rules, which ensure that investments are appropriate for a client's needs.

One of the most important aspects of this section is FINRA Rule 2111, which requires securities representatives to perform due diligence before making recommendations. Representatives must gather and analyze key financial details, including:

- A client's financial status, including income, expenses, and net worth
- Investment objectives, such as capital preservation, growth, or income generation
- Risk tolerance, which determines how much risk the client is comfortable taking
- Time horizon, or how long the client plans to hold an investment
- Tax considerations, including whether investments should be tax-advantaged

Understanding these factors helps representatives make informed recommendations, ensuring that clients are not exposed to unnecessary risk.

This section also covers asset allocation strategies and diversification principles. Candidates must understand how to structure portfolios that minimize risk while maximizing returns. They must also be able to compare different investment products, such as stocks, bonds, mutual funds, and exchange-traded funds (ETFs), and determine which best suit a client's financial profile.

3. Providing Customers with Information About Investments, Making Suitable Recommendations, and Managing Accounts

This section makes up 32% of the exam and is one of the most comprehensive areas tested. It focuses on client interactions, the handling of accounts, and ensuring that investment transactions are conducted in a legal and ethical manner.

Candidates must demonstrate knowledge of the following topics:

- The risks and benefits of various investment products, including stocks, bonds, mutual funds, and options
- Tax implications associated with securities transactions, including capital gains and dividend taxation
- Different types of brokerage accounts, such as individual accounts, joint accounts, custodial accounts, and retirement accounts
- Margin accounts and their associated risks, including leverage, margin calls, and interest charges
- Order entry procedures and proper documentation to ensure regulatory compliance

Additionally, this section includes topics related to record-keeping and transaction processing. Securities representatives must maintain accurate records of client interactions, investment recommendations, and trade executions. This is crucial for regulatory oversight and for protecting both the client and the firm from potential disputes.

Another important aspect covered in this section is handling client complaints. FINRA regulations require firms to keep a record of all complaints and address them according to industry guidelines. Securities professionals must ensure that complaints are handled professionally and in accordance with established policies.

4. Executing Trades and Ensuring Compliance with Industry Regulations

The largest portion of the exam, accounting for 45% of the questions, focuses on trade execution, order handling, and regulatory compliance. Since a registered securities representative's primary role involves buying and selling securities, this section tests a candidate's ability to execute trades accurately and efficiently.

Candidates must understand the different types of securities orders, including:

- Market orders, which are executed immediately at the current market price
- Limit orders, which specify a price at which the trade must be executed
- Stop-loss orders, which trigger a sale if the price falls below a certain level
- Short selling, where an investor borrows and sells securities in anticipation of a price decline

The exam also covers the role of market makers, the importance of bid-ask spreads, and how securities transactions are cleared and settled. Understanding the mechanisms of the financial markets is essential for ensuring that trades are executed properly and in the best interest of clients.

Another critical topic in this section is regulatory compliance. SEC Rule 10b-5, for example, prohibits fraudulent and manipulative practices in securities trading. Candidates must be familiar with anti-fraud regulations, insider trading rules, and the penalties associated with violating industry laws.

This section also addresses the responsibilities of securities professionals in reporting suspicious activities and ensuring that firms adhere to Anti-Money Laundering (AML) laws. FINRA requires firms to have procedures in place for detecting and preventing fraudulent activities, making compliance a crucial part of the exam.

PASSING SCORE AND TEST-TAKING RULES

Passing the Series 7 Exam requires a solid grasp of all key topics, strong test-taking strategies, and careful attention to FINRA's testing rules. Candidates must meet specific requirements to be eligible for the exam, follow strict rules during the test, and achieve a minimum passing score to obtain their license.

Minimum Passing Score

The Series 7 Exam consists of 125 multiple-choice questions, and candidates are given 225 minutes (3 hours and 45 minutes) to complete it. The passing score is 72%, meaning candidates must correctly answer at least 90 out of 125 questions.

While the passing score is achievable with proper preparation, the exam is challenging due to the broad range of topics covered. Questions often test not just factual knowledge but also the ability to apply financial concepts to real-world scenarios.

Candidates who do not pass the exam on their first attempt must wait 30 days before retaking it. If a candidate fails the exam three times, they must wait six months before attempting it again. These waiting periods are enforced by FINRA to ensure that candidates take the necessary time to improve their understanding before reattempting the test.

Test-Taking Rules and Regulations

The Series 7 Exam is administered at Prometric testing centers, which are authorized by FINRA to conduct securities licensing exams. Candidates must adhere to strict rules during the exam to maintain the integrity of the testing process.

To take the Series 7 Exam, candidates must:

- Be sponsored by a FINRA-member firm
- Have passed the Securities Industry Essentials (SIE) Exam
- Register for the exam through FINRA's Central Registration Depository (CRD)
- Pay the $300 exam fee (subject to change based on FINRA's updates)

Once registered, candidates can schedule their exam at a Prometric testing center, where they will take the test on a computer.

At the testing center, candidates must follow strict procedures to prevent cheating or misconduct. These include:

- Presenting valid government-issued identification
- Storing personal belongings in a designated area before entering the exam room
- Following all instructions from test center staff
- Avoiding any form of communication with other test-takers during the exam

The testing room is monitored by proctors and security cameras to ensure compliance with FINRA's rules. Any attempt to cheat, share exam content, or engage in misconduct can result in disqualification and disciplinary action.

The exam consists of 125 questions, with four answer choices for each question. Some questions may require calculations, while others test candidates on regulations, investment strategies, and ethical considerations.

Since candidates have 225 minutes to complete the exam, time management is crucial. It is recommended that candidates:

- Allocate 1.5 minutes per question
- Skip and return to difficult questions if necessary
- Use the process of elimination to narrow down answer choices

Once the exam is completed, candidates receive their scores immediately. The score report will indicate whether they passed or failed, but it will not provide a breakdown of performance on individual topics.

If a candidate passes, they will move forward in obtaining their Series 7 license. If they do not pass, they must follow FINRA's waiting period rules before attempting the exam again.

The Series 7 Exam is a significant step toward becoming a licensed securities representative. It covers a wide range of financial topics and requires candidates to apply their knowledge in real-world situations. Achieving a passing score of 72% requires strong preparation, effective study habits, and a solid understanding of test-taking rules.

CHAPTER 2
REGISTRATION AND PREPARATION

HOW TO REGISTER FOR THE EXAM (FINRA REQUIREMENTS)

The Series 7 Exam is a crucial step for anyone seeking to work as a general securities representative in the financial industry. However, before a candidate can sit for the exam, they must fulfill Financial Industry Regulatory Authority (FINRA) requirements, complete the registration process, and receive approval to take the test.

FINRA is the governing body responsible for regulating brokerage firms and securities professionals in the United States. The Series 7 Exam is part of FINRA's effort to ensure that registered representatives have the necessary knowledge and skills to operate in the securities industry while following regulatory guidelines.

To register for the Series 7 Exam, candidates must go through a structured process that includes eligibility verification, sponsorship by a FINRA-member firm, and completion of the required forms.

1. Meeting Eligibility Requirements

Before applying for the Series 7 Exam, candidates must ensure that they meet FINRA's eligibility requirements. Unlike the Securities Industry Essentials (SIE) Exam, which is open to anyone interested in the securities industry, the Series 7 Exam requires candidates to be employed by a FINRA-member firm or a self-regulatory organization (SRO).

Sponsorship by a FINRA-registered firm is mandatory because the Series 7 license allows professionals to trade securities on behalf of clients. Since securities trading involves financial risk and regulatory oversight, FINRA requires candidates to work under the supervision of a licensed brokerage firm before obtaining their own registration.

Additionally, candidates must have passed the SIE Exam before taking the Series 7 Exam. The SIE Exam serves as an introductory test, covering foundational topics such as financial markets, investment products, and regulatory rules. While the SIE Exam does not require firm sponsorship, it is a prerequisite for taking the Series 7 Exam.

Another crucial aspect of eligibility is FINRA's background check process. Candidates must submit detailed information about their employment history, legal background, and financial history. Any past criminal convictions, financial misconduct, or regulatory violations may disqualify an individual from registering as a securities representative.

2. Securing Sponsorship from a FINRA-Member Firm

Securing sponsorship from a FINRA-member firm is a crucial step in the registration process. Sponsorship ensures that candidates are working under the supervision of an established brokerage firm, investment bank, or securities firm that complies with FINRA regulations.

Sponsoring firms play an important role in:

- Registering candidates with FINRA and ensuring they meet regulatory requirements
- Providing on-the-job training for securities trading and customer interactions
- Monitoring compliance and ethical behavior in financial transactions

Most candidates secure sponsorship by applying for entry-level positions at brokerage firms, investment banks, or wealth management firms. Many large financial firms offer training programs designed to prepare new employees for the Series 7 Exam. These programs typically provide structured study plans, mentorship, and exam preparation resources.

Once a candidate is hired, the sponsoring firm initiates the registration process by submitting the necessary paperwork to FINRA.

3. Completing and Submitting Form U4

Once a candidate has secured sponsorship, the next step is submitting Form U4 (Uniform Application for Securities Industry Registration or Transfer). This form is a mandatory requirement for individuals seeking registration with FINRA and is used to collect important background information.

Form U4 includes:

- Personal information (name, address, date of birth, and Social Security number)
- Employment history (previous jobs, roles in the financial industry, and relevant experience)
- Educational background (degree information, certifications, and financial training)
- Legal disclosures (criminal history, regulatory violations, and disciplinary actions)

Because securities professionals handle client investments, FINRA conducts a thorough background check based on the information provided in Form U4. If a candidate has a history of financial fraud, unethical behavior, or criminal activity, they may be disqualified from obtaining a securities license.

The sponsoring firm is responsible for submitting Form U4 electronically through FINRA's Central Registration Depository (CRD) system. Once the form is approved, the candidate is officially registered to take the Series 7 Exam.

4. Paying the Exam Fee and Scheduling the Test

After submitting Form U4, candidates must pay the Series 7 Exam fee, which is currently $300. This non-refundable fee must be paid before scheduling the test. Since FINRA may update exam fees periodically, candidates should check FINRA's website for the latest pricing information.

Once the exam fee is paid, candidates can schedule their test through Prometric, the official testing provider for FINRA exams. Prometric has testing centers across the country, and candidates can choose a convenient location and exam date.

On exam day, candidates must bring a valid government-issued ID and follow all testing center rules. Personal items, notes, and electronic devices are not allowed in the exam room. The test is computer-based, and candidates receive their results immediately upon completion.

CHOOSING THE RIGHT STUDY MATERIALS

With various study materials available, it is essential to choose those that match an individual's learning style, experience, and study preferences. Some candidates prefer structured textbooks and study guides, while others benefit from interactive video courses or mobile-based tools. Many successful test-takers use a combination of resources, such as textbooks for in-depth understanding, practice exams for testing knowledge, and flashcards for quick recall of important concepts. The right selection of study materials can significantly impact a candidate's performance on exam day.

1. FINRA's Official Exam Content Outline

FINRA's official Series 7 Exam Content Outline is one of the most important resources for candidates. This document provides a comprehensive roadmap of the exam, outlining the topics covered and their respective weightage. Since FINRA periodically updates the exam structure to align with changes in industry regulations, candidates should always refer to the latest version of the content outline to ensure they are studying the correct material.

The content outline serves as a guide for structuring study sessions, helping candidates allocate their time effectively based on topic importance. Some sections carry more weight in the exam, such as those covering trading and order execution, meaning candidates should devote extra time to mastering those topics. Many candidates make the mistake of ignoring the content outline and relying solely on third-party study guides. However, using the outline alongside study materials ensures that all key areas are covered, reducing the risk of missing important concepts.

Another advantage of using FINRA's content outline is that it provides a breakdown of regulatory rules and ethical guidelines tested in the exam. Since a significant portion of the Series 7 Exam focuses on compliance, understanding these regulations in detail is essential. Candidates can use the outline to cross-reference study materials and verify that they are reviewing the most relevant laws and industry standards.

2. Study Guides and Textbooks

Study guides and textbooks are essential tools for mastering the Series 7 Exam. These resources offer structured explanations of key topics, allowing candidates to build a solid foundation in securities trading and financial regulations. A well-structured textbook simplifies complex concepts, providing real-world examples and practice exercises that help reinforce learning.

Several reputable publishers offer Series 7 study guides designed specifically for exam preparation. Kaplan, Pass Perfect, Wiley, and Securities Training Corporation (STC) provide some of the most widely used books in the industry. These textbooks cover all sections of the exam in a step-by-step format, with detailed explanations of securities products, investment strategies, and ethical considerations. Many study guides also include review sections and chapter quizzes that allow candidates to assess their progress as they go through the material.

When selecting a study guide, candidates should consider books that align with their learning style. Some books focus on detailed explanations, while others are designed for quick review and high-level summaries. Candidates who struggle with certain topics should opt for comprehensive textbooks with in-depth analysis, whereas those who already have a background in finance may benefit from condensed study materials that focus on exam-specific content.

Textbooks should be supplemented with additional resources, such as online practice questions or video explanations. Since reading alone may not be enough to retain complex information, combining textbooks with interactive learning tools can improve retention and comprehension. Additionally, candidates should ensure they are using the latest edition of a study guide, as securities laws and FINRA regulations are subject to change.

3. Online Courses and Video Lectures

For candidates who prefer a more interactive learning experience, online courses and video lectures offer an excellent alternative to traditional textbooks. Many test-takers find video-based learning more engaging, as it allows them to absorb information through visual and auditory explanations. Online courses break down complex Series 7 topics into manageable lessons, often including animations, real-world examples, and instructor-led discussions.

Several financial education providers offer online Series 7 training programs, including Kaplan, Knopman Marks, ExamFX, and

Securities Training Corporation (STC). These courses provide structured lesson plans, covering all exam topics in an organized manner. Some platforms offer live online classes, where candidates can interact with instructors and ask questions in real-time. Others provide on-demand video lectures, allowing candidates to study at their own pace.

One of the biggest advantages of online courses is that they often include additional study resources, such as digital flashcards, practice exams, and interactive quizzes. These tools help reinforce learning and allow candidates to track their progress as they move through the course. Many courses also include mobile compatibility, enabling candidates to study on the go.

For individuals who struggle with self-study, enrolling in an online Series 7 boot camp or coaching program may be beneficial. These intensive programs provide structured learning schedules and personalized support from instructors, ensuring candidates stay on track with their preparation. Some boot camps even offer one-on-one tutoring sessions, where candidates can receive targeted assistance on their weak areas.

4. Practice Exams and Question Banks

Taking practice exams is one of the most effective ways to prepare for the Series 7 Exam. Since the test consists of multiple-choice questions, practicing with real exam-style questions helps candidates familiarize themselves with the format, improve time management, and identify areas for improvement. Many candidates who pass the Series 7 Exam emphasize that practice exams played a crucial role in their preparation.

Most study providers offer question banks that contain thousands of practice questions, simulating real exam conditions. These questions help reinforce knowledge by testing candidates on investment principles, securities regulations, and client suitability. Some of the best Series 7 practice question banks come from Kaplan, Pass Perfect, STC, and Wiley.

One of the key benefits of using practice exams is that they allow candidates to assess their readiness before the real test. Many question banks provide performance tracking tools, showing candidates which topics they need to improve. Taking full-length timed exams also helps candidates develop test-taking strategies, such as how to pace themselves and avoid spending too much time on difficult questions.

Candidates should aim to complete at least five to six full-length practice exams before sitting for the real test. This will help build confidence and improve accuracy under exam conditions. Reviewing incorrect answers and understanding why they were wrong is just as important as taking the tests themselves.

5. Flashcards and Memory Aids

Since the Series 7 Exam requires memorization of investment terms, regulatory rules, and financial formulas, using flashcards can be an effective study method. Flashcards help reinforce important information through active recall, allowing candidates to quiz themselves on key concepts.

Many financial education providers offer Series 7 flashcards, available in both physical and digital formats. Kaplan, Brainscape, and Quizlet have extensive flashcard decks covering all exam topics. Candidates can also create their own custom flashcards to focus on specific areas they find challenging.

Flashcards are particularly useful for memorizing securities laws, key financial ratios, and margin account requirements. Since flashcards are easy to carry, candidates can use them for quick review sessions throughout the day. This method is especially beneficial for individuals with busy schedules, as it allows for efficient studying during breaks or commutes.

6. Mobile Apps and Study Tools

For candidates who prefer studying on the go, mobile apps and digital study tools provide a convenient way to prepare for the Series 7 Exam. Many financial education providers have developed mobile-friendly applications that include practice questions, mini-quizzes, and topic summaries. These apps allow candidates to integrate study sessions into their daily routine without requiring dedicated study time.

Popular Series 7 study apps include Achievable, Securities Institute of America's mobile app, and Kaplan's Pocket Prep. These apps provide bite-sized learning modules, performance tracking, and adaptive learning features that help candidates strengthen their weak areas.

Another benefit of using study apps is that they offer daily reminders and progress tracking, keeping candidates accountable for their study goals. Many apps also feature gamification elements, such as earning rewards for completing quizzes, which can make studying more engaging.

Selecting the right study materials is a critical step in passing the Series 7 Exam. Candidates should use a combination of study guides, online courses, practice exams, flashcards, and mobile tools to create a comprehensive preparation strategy. Since the exam tests both theoretical knowledge and practical application, using multiple resources ensures that candidates fully understand the material and are well-prepared for test day.

SETTING UP A STUDY SCHEDULE

Preparing for the Series 7 Exam requires a well-structured and disciplined study approach. Given the exam's extensive coverage of securities products, regulations, and trading strategies, candidates must develop an effective study schedule that allows them to thoroughly review all necessary material while balancing work and personal commitments. Without a structured plan, studying can become overwhelming, leading to inefficient preparation, last-minute cramming, and potential failure on exam day.

A strategic study schedule helps candidates stay organized, track progress, and allocate sufficient time to challenging topics. The amount of time needed to prepare for the Series 7 Exam varies based on an individual's background in finance, work experience, and familiarity with securities laws and trading principles. On average, candidates spend 80 to 150 hours preparing, which translates to about four to eight weeks of study time if approached consistently.

Creating a study schedule tailored to personal learning preferences and availability is essential for success. This section provides a detailed guide on how to create a structured and effective study plan, ensuring candidates cover all key topics, maintain retention, and build confidence before the exam.

1. Determining the Total Study Time Needed

Before setting up a study schedule, candidates must first determine how much time they need to prepare. The recommended study duration varies based on prior knowledge and experience in finance.

For candidates with experience in the financial industry, such as those working in brokerage firms, investment banking, or wealth management, preparation time may range from four to six weeks, dedicating 10 to 15 hours per week to studying. Since these individuals already have familiarity with trading concepts and regulations, they can focus more on exam-specific strategies and practice questions.

For candidates with little to no background in securities or finance, a more extensive study plan is required. These individuals should allocate six to eight weeks of preparation time, studying for 15 to 20 hours per week to ensure they grasp all key concepts. Given the complexity of securities laws, investment strategies, and risk management principles, additional time will be needed for memorization and practice exams.

Candidates must also consider their work schedules, personal commitments, and study efficiency when deciding the number of hours per week they can realistically dedicate to exam preparation. A study schedule should be achievable and consistent, ensuring steady progress over time without causing burnout.

2. Dividing the Study Plan into Phases

Breaking the study schedule into phases helps create a systematic learning approach. The Series 7 Exam covers a broad range of topics, and attempting to study everything at once can be overwhelming. A structured plan typically consists of three main phases:

Phase 1: Core Learning (Weeks 1-3 or 1-4, depending on timeline)

The first phase focuses on understanding core concepts and building a solid foundation. During this stage, candidates should dedicate time to reading textbooks, watching video lectures, and taking notes. The goal is to become familiar with investment products, market regulations, trading strategies, and client suitability requirements.

A study plan in this phase should allocate one to two hours per day, focusing on one topic at a time. Candidates should avoid rushing through material and instead aim for deep comprehension. Using study guides, online courses, and flashcards can be helpful for retaining key concepts.

Phase 2: Practice and Reinforcement (Weeks 4-6 or 5-7, depending on timeline)

After building a foundation, the second phase should shift focus toward application and practice. This involves working through practice exams, question banks, and scenario-based case studies to develop test-taking strategies. Since the Series 7 Exam consists of multiple-choice questions that test concept application rather than simple memorization, practicing with exam-style questions is crucial for success.

Candidates should aim to complete at least 50 to 100 practice questions per study session, analyzing mistakes and reviewing incorrect answers. This helps identify weak areas that require further review. Revisiting study guides and notes during this phase reinforces understanding of challenging topics.

Phase 3: Full-Length Exams and Review (Final Week or Two Weeks Before Exam)

The final phase focuses on full-length mock exams and last-minute reviews. Candidates should attempt at least three to five full-length simulated exams under real exam conditions. Timed practice helps improve time management skills, ensuring candidates can complete the 125-question exam within the 225-minute limit.

During this phase, candidates should prioritize weak areas identified in previous practice tests. Reviewing summary notes, flashcards, and revisiting difficult concepts ensures retention. The final week should be used for light revision and mental preparation, avoiding cramming to reduce test anxiety.

3. Allocating Time for Each Exam Topic

Since different topics carry different weight in the Series 7 Exam, candidates should allocate more study time to high-weightage sections while ensuring adequate coverage of all topics. The exam is divided into four major areas, each requiring different levels of attention. Given this distribution, candidates should dedicate at least 40-50% of their study time to mastering trading execution, regulatory compliance, and investment suitability. The remaining time should be allocated proportionally to the other sections based on their weightage.

4. Scheduling Study Sessions for Maximum Retention

Creating a consistent study routine is crucial for retention and recall. Studies show that spaced repetition and active learning techniques enhance memory and comprehension. Instead of cramming large amounts of material at once, candidates should spread out study sessions over multiple weeks, reviewing information multiple times.

The most effective study schedules incorporate daily learning blocks of 1.5 to 3 hours, divided as follows:

- First 45 minutes to 1 hour: Reading and understanding new material
- Next 30 minutes to 1 hour: Practicing questions related to the topic studied
- Final 15-30 minutes: Reviewing mistakes and reinforcing key takeaways

Additionally, weekly review sessions should be included to summarize concepts covered throughout the week. This helps ensure long-term retention and prevents forgetting previously studied material.

5. Incorporating Breaks and Avoiding Burnout

A common mistake candidates make is overloading their study schedule, leading to burnout and decreased productivity. Long, uninterrupted study sessions can cause mental fatigue, making it harder to absorb and retain information.

To maintain study efficiency, candidates should incorporate breaks between study sessions. The Pomodoro technique, which involves 25-50 minutes of focused studying followed by a short

5-10 minute break, can enhance concentration and prevent burnout. Longer breaks (30-60 minutes) should be scheduled after intensive study sessions or full-length practice exams to allow for mental recovery.

A study schedule should be flexible and adjustable based on progress and changing commitments. If certain topics prove to be more difficult than expected, candidates should allocate additional study time to those areas.

Tracking progress through self-assessments, quizzes, and practice exams can help identify weak areas early. Candidates who consistently struggle with specific concepts should revisit study guides, seek clarification through online courses, or consider working with a tutor.

As the exam date approaches, the study schedule should shift toward revision, reinforcement, and mental preparation, rather than introducing new concepts.

TEST-TAKING STRATEGIES

Many candidates who are well-prepared still struggle on exam day due to poor test-taking strategies, such as spending too much time on difficult questions, second-guessing their answers, or becoming overwhelmed by the pressure of the exam environment. To maximize performance, candidates need to develop a systematic approach to answering questions, managing time, and staying focused throughout the test.

Understanding the Exam Format and Question Types

Before entering the exam, candidates must have a clear understanding of the test format and the different types of questions they will encounter. The Series 7 Exam consists of multiple-choice questions, each with four answer choices. While some questions test straightforward knowledge, others require application-based thinking and involve client scenarios, financial calculations, and regulatory considerations.

The exam features fact-based questions that assess direct knowledge of regulations, definitions, and financial concepts. These are usually straightforward and test whether candidates have memorized key details. Scenario-based questions present a hypothetical client situation and ask candidates to determine the best course of action. These questions assess an individual's ability to apply investment suitability principles, risk assessment, and regulatory compliance. Additionally, some questions require basic calculations, such as determining bond yields, margin requirements, or investment returns. While the math involved is not complex, candidates must be comfortable with financial formulas and problem-solving techniques.

Understanding these question types helps candidates anticipate how to approach each question, ensuring they do not waste unnecessary time analyzing simpler fact-based items while prioritizing more complex scenario-based and calculation-based questions.

Managing Time Effectively

Time management is one of the most critical aspects of passing the Series 7 Exam. With 125 questions to complete in 225 minutes, candidates have approximately 1.8 minutes per question. However, since some questions are more complex than others, candidates should aim to complete simpler questions quickly to allow more time for the challenging ones.

One of the best strategies for time management is the first-pass approach. This involves going through the exam and answering all the questions that can be completed quickly and confidently. If a question appears difficult or time-consuming, candidates should flag it and move on to the next one. Once all easy questions are completed, they can return to the flagged questions and dedicate more time to them.

Another effective technique is time-checking. Candidates should set time benchmarks throughout the exam to ensure they are on track. For example, they should aim to complete 40 questions in the first 70 minutes, 80 questions by the 140-minute mark, and finish the remaining 45 questions in the last 85 minutes. This approach prevents last-minute rushing and ensures that there is sufficient time to review flagged questions at the end.

Practicing full-length timed exams before the test date is also essential for improving time management. Candidates should simulate real exam conditions by completing practice tests within the allotted time. This helps them get accustomed to pacing and recognize which types of questions tend to consume the most time.

Using the Process of Elimination

One of the most effective test-taking strategies is using the process of elimination to narrow down answer choices. Since each question on the Series 7 Exam has four possible answers, eliminating incorrect choices increases the likelihood of selecting the right one.

The first step in eliminating incorrect answers is identifying responses that are clearly wrong. Sometimes, an answer choice will contradict basic financial principles or regulatory guidelines. If a choice seems extreme, overly risky, or does not align with industry regulations, it can often be ruled out immediately.

Another elimination method is looking for answers that are too similar. Occasionally, two of the four answer choices may be nearly identical, differing only slightly in wording. In such cases, one of them is likely correct. Candidates should closely examine these choices and determine which one best aligns with the exam content they have studied.

For scenario-based questions, candidates should analyze the client's profile before selecting an answer. Many questions present a hypothetical client situation and require candidates to determine the most suitable investment recommendation. If a client is described as risk-averse, any answer choice that involves high-risk investments, such as options trading or speculative stocks, can likely be eliminated.

If candidates are unsure of an answer after eliminating incorrect choices, they should make an educated guess rather than leaving it blank. Since there is no penalty for guessing, answering all questions increases the chances of earning additional points.

Avoiding Overthinking and Second-Guessing Answers

Overthinking is one of the most common pitfalls on the Series 7 Exam. Many candidates second-guess their answers and change them, often switching from the correct response to an incorrect one. While it is important to review flagged questions at the end of the exam, excessive second-guessing can lead to unnecessary mistakes.

A good rule of thumb is to trust the initial instinct unless there is a clear reason to change an answer. Research on test-taking strategies suggests that the first answer choice a test-taker selects is often correct, especially if they have prepared well. If a candidate finds themselves hesitating over a question they previously answered confidently, they should stick with their original response unless they recall new information that contradicts it.

To minimize overthinking, candidates should focus on reading questions carefully before answering. Misreading a question or overlooking key details can lead to unnecessary errors. If a question seems unclear, reading it twice and underlining important words or numbers can help in identifying the correct response.

Handling Calculation-Based Questions Efficiently

While the Series 7 Exam does not heavily emphasize mathematical calculations, there are several questions that require financial problem-solving. These may involve determining bond yields, margin requirements, or profit-and-loss calculations. Candidates should be comfortable with basic financial formulas and know when to apply them.

One of the best strategies for handling calculation-based questions is writing out key numbers and formulas before attempting to solve the problem. Since the exam is computer-based, candidates will be provided with a physical notepad or scratch paper at the testing center. Writing down the given figures and setting up the equation properly can prevent careless mistakes.

Additionally, candidates should not spend excessive time on any single math question. If a calculation appears too complex or time-consuming, it is better to flag the question and return to it later. Since only a small percentage of the exam involves calculations, it is important to ensure that these questions do not take time away from the rest of the test.

Practicing financial calculations before the exam can help improve efficiency. Candidates should work through sample problems involving interest rates, bond yields, and option pricing to become familiar with the types of math questions that may appear on the test.

Staying Calm and Managing Test Anxiety

Test anxiety is a common challenge for many candidates taking the Series 7 Exam. The pressure of a high-stakes test, combined with the long exam duration, can lead to nervousness and mental fatigue. However, developing strategies to stay calm and focused can significantly improve performance.

One effective method for managing test anxiety is practicing relaxation techniques before and during the exam. Deep breathing exercises, visualization, and mindfulness can help candidates stay composed under pressure. If a candidate starts feeling overwhelmed, taking a few deep breaths and refocusing on the question at hand can prevent anxiety from escalating.

Maintaining a steady pace throughout the exam is also important for reducing stress. Rushing through questions increases the risk of careless mistakes, while spending too much time on a single question can create unnecessary pressure. By following a well-structured time management plan, candidates can maintain a sense of control and confidence.

Getting a good night's sleep before the exam is another crucial factor in managing test anxiety. Lack of sleep can impair concentration, memory, and decision-making abilities, making it harder to recall important concepts. Eating a healthy meal before the test and staying hydrated can also help maintain energy levels and mental clarity during the exam.

PART 2

CORE CONCEPTS AND TOPICS

CHAPTER 3

EQUITY SECURITIES

COMMON STOCKS

Ownership and Voting Rights

When investors purchase common stock, they become partial owners of the company. This ownership grants them certain rights, the most significant of which is voting power. Common stockholders typically have the right to vote on major corporate matters, including electing members of the board of directors, approving mergers and acquisitions, and making significant company policy decisions. Each share of common stock generally represents one vote, though some companies issue multiple classes of stock with different voting rights. These dual-class structures allow founders and executives to maintain control over a company even if they own a smaller percentage of total outstanding shares.

Voting rights are exercised at annual shareholder meetings, where investors can either attend in person or vote by proxy. While individual investors may not have enough shares to influence corporate decisions significantly, institutional investors such as mutual funds and pension funds can have considerable sway over a company's direction due to their large stock holdings. In some cases, activist investors use their voting power to push for changes in company management or strategic direction.

Capital Appreciation Potential

One of the primary reasons investors buy common stock is the potential for capital appreciation. As a company grows and generates higher earnings, its stock price tends to increase, allowing investors to sell their shares at a profit. Over the long term, common stocks have outperformed most other asset classes, making them a popular investment for those seeking wealth accumulation.

Stock prices are influenced by several factors, including a company's financial performance, economic conditions, industry trends, and overall market sentiment. Companies that consistently report strong revenue growth and profitability often experience rising stock prices, while firms that struggle financially may see their stock values decline. Investors rely on various analytical methods, including fundamental analysis and technical analysis, to assess a stock's potential for future appreciation.

Growth stocks, which belong to companies that are expanding rapidly, typically reinvest profits into the business rather than paying dividends. These stocks tend to experience substantial price appreciation over time, making them attractive to investors with a higher risk tolerance. On the other hand, value stocks trade at prices lower than their intrinsic worth and are favored by investors who believe the market has undervalued the company's true potential.

Dividend Payments

While common stocks do not guarantee dividends, many companies choose to distribute a portion of their earnings to shareholders in the form of cash payments. Dividends provide investors with a steady income stream and can enhance total investment returns over time. Companies that pay dividends are usually well-established and financially stable, as they generate consistent profits that allow them to share earnings with investors.

Dividend payments are determined by a company's board of directors and can be increased, decreased, or suspended based on financial performance and business needs. Unlike bond interest payments, which are contractual obligations, companies are not required to pay dividends on common stock. In times of economic downturns or financial instability, companies may choose to reduce or eliminate dividends to preserve capital.

There are different types of dividend-paying stocks. Blue-chip stocks, which belong to large, well-established companies, often provide reliable dividend payments. Dividend growth stocks, on the other hand, are those that consistently increase their dividends over time, making them attractive to long-term investors seeking both income and capital appreciation. Some investors specifically target high-dividend-yield stocks to generate passive income, while others focus on companies that reinvest earnings for future growth rather than paying out dividends.

Market Volatility and Risk Factors

Common stocks are subject to market volatility, meaning their prices can fluctuate widely due to economic conditions, company performance, industry trends, and investor sentiment.

Unlike fixed-income securities such as bonds, common stocks do not offer guaranteed returns, making them inherently riskier investments. However, this higher level of risk comes with the potential for greater long-term rewards.

Several factors contribute to stock price volatility. Economic indicators such as interest rates, inflation, and GDP growth impact overall market conditions. When interest rates rise, borrowing costs increase, which can reduce corporate profits and negatively affect stock prices. Inflation can erode purchasing power and decrease consumer spending, leading to lower revenue for businesses. Additionally, company-specific factors such as earnings reports, management changes, and industry competition can cause fluctuations in a stock's value.

Investors must consider their risk tolerance when investing in common stocks. While younger investors with long investment horizons may be more willing to endure short-term price fluctuations for long-term gains, retirees and conservative investors may prefer less volatile assets. Diversification, or spreading investments across different sectors and asset classes, can help mitigate risk by reducing exposure to individual stock declines.

Liquidation Priority and Residual Claims

In the event of a company's liquidation or bankruptcy, common stockholders are last in line to receive compensation. When a company is forced to dissolve its assets, its obligations to creditors, bondholders, and preferred stockholders must be satisfied before any remaining funds are distributed to common stockholders. In many cases, common stockholders receive little to no compensation after all debts and senior claims have been settled.

This liquidation priority makes common stocks riskier than preferred stocks and bonds, which have a higher claim on a company's assets. However, the higher risk associated with common stock is balanced by the potential for greater capital appreciation and long-term wealth accumulation. While preferred stockholders receive fixed dividends and have a better claim in the event of liquidation, they do not benefit from the same level of stock price growth as common stockholders.

PREFERRED STOCKS

Preferred stock is a unique hybrid security that shares characteristics of both common stock and bonds. It represents ownership in a company but typically provides a fixed dividend payment, similar to the interest payments on a bond. Because of this fixed income component, preferred stocks are often considered less volatile than common stocks and are popular among income-focused investors.

One of the key advantages of preferred stock is that it has a higher claim on company assets and earnings than common stock. In the event of liquidation, preferred stockholders are paid before common stockholders, although they still rank below creditors and bondholders. Additionally, preferred stock dividends must be paid before any dividends are distributed to common stockholders.

Despite offering more stability, preferred stocks do not provide the same capital appreciation potential as common stocks. They also generally lack voting rights, meaning preferred shareholders do not have a say in corporate governance decisions. Some preferred stocks come with additional features, such as convertibility, which allows investors to convert their shares into common stock under specific conditions.

Preferred stocks are commonly issued by financial institutions and utility companies, which value the ability to raise capital while maintaining stable dividend distributions. Investors who prioritize steady income over growth potential often allocate a portion of their portfolios to preferred stocks, as they offer higher yields than bonds while maintaining lower volatility than common stocks.

Both common and preferred stocks play essential roles in the financial markets. While common stocks offer higher potential returns and voting rights, preferred stocks provide greater stability and income predictability. Investors must weigh the risks and benefits of each security type when building their portfolios to align with their financial goals and risk tolerance.

STOCK VALUATION AND PRICING

Stock valuation and pricing are fundamental concepts in investing, as they help determine the true worth of a company's shares. Understanding how stocks are valued allows investors to make informed decisions about buying, holding, or selling a stock. Since stock prices fluctuate based on a variety of factors, valuation methods help investors distinguish between a stock's market price and its intrinsic value—the actual worth of the stock based on financial performance, growth potential, and industry conditions.

Stocks are priced in the market based on supply and demand, which is influenced by investor sentiment, earnings reports, economic conditions, and external factors such as political stability and central bank policies. However, the market price of a stock does not always reflect its true value. The stock market is subject to speculation, and stocks may be overvalued or undervalued at any given time. This is why investors use different valuation techniques to assess whether a stock is fairly priced, overpriced, or undervalued.

There are two primary approaches to stock valuation: fundamental analysis and technical analysis. Fundamental analysis focuses on a company's financial health, earnings, growth potential, and competitive position, while technical analysis evaluates historical price movements, trading volumes, and market trends to predict future stock prices. Each method has its advantages and limitations, and many investors use a combination of both approaches to develop a well-rounded investment strategy.

Intrinsic Value vs. Market Price

The concept of intrinsic value is central to stock valuation. Intrinsic value represents what a stock is truly worth, based on its underlying financials and growth potential. This differs from the market price, which is the price at which a stock is currently trading on an exchange. The market price fluctuates based on investor demand, speculation, and macroeconomic factors, but it does not always reflect a stock's real worth.

When a stock's intrinsic value is higher than its market price, the stock is considered undervalued and may represent a good buying opportunity. Conversely, if a stock's intrinsic value is lower than its market price, it is considered overvalued, and investors may avoid it or sell their existing holdings.

Different valuation models attempt to determine intrinsic value using financial statements, projected earnings, cash flows, and industry comparisons. While these models are not perfect, they help investors estimate a stock's fair value relative to its market price.

Fundamental Analysis and Stock Valuation

Fundamental analysis is the most widely used method for valuing stocks. It involves analyzing a company's financial health, industry position, competitive advantages, and economic factors to determine its true worth. Fundamental analysis is used by long-term investors who seek to invest in companies with strong business models, sustainable earnings, and growth potential.

One of the primary components of fundamental analysis is examining a company's financial statements, including the income statement, balance sheet, and cash flow statement. These documents provide key insights into a company's revenue, profitability, assets, liabilities, and cash flow. Investors and analysts use these metrics to determine whether a company is financially stable and capable of generating long-term growth.

Profitability ratios such as earnings per share (EPS), return on equity (ROE), and net profit margin are essential in assessing a company's ability to generate profits from its operations. Liquidity and debt ratios, such as the current ratio and debt-to-equity ratio, help investors understand whether a company can meet its short-term and long-term obligations.

Another important aspect of fundamental analysis is evaluating a company's growth potential. Investors look at a company's historical earnings growth, projected revenue growth, and expansion plans to estimate its future performance. Companies that consistently grow their earnings over time tend to have higher stock valuations, as they are expected to generate strong returns for shareholders.

Valuation Methods in Fundamental Analysis

Several financial models are used in fundamental analysis to determine a stock's intrinsic value. The most common valuation methods include the price-to-earnings (P/E) ratio, discounted cash flow (DCF) analysis, and price-to-book (P/B) ratio.

The P/E ratio compares a company's stock price to its earnings per share. It is one of the most widely used valuation metrics, as it helps investors assess how much they are paying for a company's earnings. A high P/E ratio may indicate that a stock is overvalued, while a low P/E ratio may suggest that a stock is undervalued. However, P/E ratios vary across industries, so investors must compare a company's P/E ratio with industry averages to get a clearer picture.

The discounted cash flow (DCF) model is a more complex valuation method that estimates a company's intrinsic value by projecting its future cash flows and discounting them to the present value. The idea behind DCF analysis is that a stock is worth the present value of all its future cash flows, adjusted for risk and time value of money. This method requires making assumptions about future revenue, expenses, growth rates, and discount rates. While DCF analysis is powerful, it can be highly sensitive to assumptions, making it important for investors to use realistic projections.

The price-to-book (P/B) ratio compares a company's stock price to its book value, which is the value of its assets minus liabilities. This ratio helps investors assess whether a stock is trading above or below its net asset value. A P/B ratio below 1 may indicate an undervalued stock, while a P/B ratio above 1 suggests that investors are willing to pay a premium for the company's future growth potential.

Technical Analysis and Stock Pricing

Unlike fundamental analysis, which focuses on financial statements and business performance, technical analysis evaluates historical stock price movements and trading patterns to predict future price behavior. Technical analysts believe that stock prices reflect all available information, and that price trends and market sentiment can be used to make investment decisions.

Technical analysis relies on price charts, technical indicators, and volume data to identify potential buying and selling opportunities. Some of the most commonly used tools in technical analysis include moving averages, relative strength index (RSI), Bollinger Bands, and MACD (moving average convergence divergence).

One of the most basic technical indicators is the moving average, which smooths out price fluctuations to identify overall trends. The 50-day and 200-day moving averages are often used by traders to determine whether a stock is in an uptrend or downtrend. If a stock's price is consistently above its moving average, it is considered to be in an upward trend, while a price below the moving average suggests a downward trend.

The relative strength index (RSI) measures the speed and change of stock price movements. RSI values range from 0 to 100, with readings above 70 indicating that a stock may be overbought and due for a price correction, while readings below 30 suggest that a stock may be oversold and due for a rebound.

Technical analysis is primarily used by short-term traders and momentum investors who seek to capitalize on price fluctuations. While it does not focus on a company's financial health, it helps traders identify entry and exit points for stocks based on past price behavior.

Market Influences on Stock Pricing

Stock prices are affected by a combination of company-specific factors and broader market conditions. Investor sentiment, macroeconomic indicators, interest rates, inflation, and geopolitical events all play a role in stock price movements.

Earnings reports, product launches, mergers and acquisitions, and changes in company leadership can significantly impact stock prices. Positive earnings surprises or strong forward guidance often lead to stock price increases, while disappointing financial results can cause sharp declines.

Interest rates set by central banks also influence stock prices. When interest rates are low, borrowing costs decrease, making it easier for companies to expand their businesses and generate higher profits. This tends to drive stock prices higher. Conversely, rising interest rates can slow economic growth and reduce corporate earnings, leading to lower stock prices.

Investor sentiment and behavioral factors, such as fear and greed, also contribute to stock price fluctuations. Bullish markets, where investors are optimistic, lead to rising stock prices, while bearish markets, driven by fear and uncertainty, result in declining stock prices.

DIVIDENDS AND STOCK SPLITS

Dividends and stock splits are two essential corporate actions that affect shareholders and influence stock prices. Dividends provide investors with a share of a company's profits, while stock splits adjust the number of outstanding shares without changing a company's total market capitalization. Both of these actions are commonly used by companies to maintain shareholder value, attract investors, and manage stock liquidity. Understanding dividends and stock splits is crucial for investors, as they impact investment returns, stock valuation, and overall portfolio strategy.

Companies that generate consistent profits often distribute a portion of their earnings to shareholders in the form of dividends. Dividends serve as a reward for investing in the company and can provide a steady income stream, especially for long-term investors who rely on dividends for passive income. On the other hand, stock splits are primarily used to adjust a stock's trading price, making shares more affordable to a broader range of investors without altering the company's fundamental value. Both dividends and stock splits have distinct implications for shareholders, market perception, and future stock performance.

Dividends

Dividends represent a company's way of sharing its earnings with investors. Not all companies pay dividends, as some prefer to reinvest their profits into business expansion, research, and acquisitions. However, many established and profitable companies choose to distribute a portion of their earnings as dividends to reward shareholders and attract income-focused investors. Dividends can be issued in various forms, with the most common being cash dividends and stock dividends.

A cash dividend is a direct payment made to shareholders, typically on a per-share basis. Companies declare a specific dividend amount per share, and investors receive payments either quarterly, semi-annually, or annually. For example, if a company declares a $2.00 annual dividend per share and an investor owns 100 shares, they will receive $200 in dividend income for the year. Cash dividends are especially popular among income-oriented investors, such as retirees who rely on dividend payments to supplement their income.

A stock dividend, on the other hand, involves issuing additional shares to existing shareholders instead of paying cash. For instance, if a company declares a 5% stock dividend, shareholders receive five additional shares for every 100 shares they own. Stock dividends increase the total number of outstanding shares while maintaining each investor's proportional ownership in the company. Unlike cash dividends, stock dividends do not provide immediate income but can result in long-term gains if the stock price appreciates.

Dividends are not guaranteed, and a company's ability to pay dividends depends on its financial health, profitability, and cash flow. During economic downturns or financial struggles, companies may reduce or suspend dividend payments to preserve capital. Conversely, companies with stable earnings and strong cash reserves often maintain or increase their dividends over time, making them attractive to long-term investors.

Dividend-paying companies are often categorized into two groups: growth companies and income-oriented companies. Growth companies, such as technology firms, typically reinvest their profits into business expansion and innovation rather than paying dividends. Income-oriented companies, such as utilities, consumer goods, and financial institutions, prioritize dividend payments to attract investors seeking steady income. Investors who focus on dividend-paying stocks often look for companies with a history of dividend growth, as increasing dividends indicate financial stability and strong future earnings potential.

Dividend Declaration and Payment Process

The process of dividend distribution follows a structured timeline, including the declaration date, ex-dividend date, record date, and payment date. Each stage is important in determining which investors qualify to receive dividends.

The declaration date is when the company's board of directors announces the dividend payment, including the dividend amount and payment schedule. This announcement signals the company's commitment to distributing earnings to shareholders.

The ex-dividend date is the cutoff date for investors to qualify for the dividend. Investors who purchase shares before the ex-dividend date are eligible to receive the dividend, while those who buy shares on or after this date are not entitled to the upcoming dividend payment. The stock price typically drops by the dividend amount on the ex-dividend date, reflecting the distribution of company earnings.

The record date is when the company officially determines which shareholders are eligible for the dividend payment. Investors must be registered as shareholders by this date to receive the dividend.

The payment date is when the company distributes dividend payments to shareholders. Investors receive dividends in their brokerage accounts or as direct deposits, depending on the company's payment method.

Dividend payments have a direct impact on stock prices. When a company announces a dividend, its stock price may rise as investors view dividends as a sign of financial strength. However, after the ex-dividend date, the stock price usually adjusts downward to account for the cash paid out to shareholders.

Dividend Yield and Payout Ratio

Investors often evaluate dividend-paying stocks based on two key metrics: the dividend yield and the dividend payout ratio. These metrics help investors assess a company's ability to sustain and grow its dividends over time.

The dividend yield is calculated by dividing the annual dividend per share by the stock's market price. It represents the percentage return an investor earns from dividends relative to the stock price. For example, if a stock trades at $50 per share and pays an annual dividend of $2, its dividend yield is 4% ($2 ÷ $50). A higher dividend yield may indicate an attractive income opportunity, but it is essential to ensure the company can maintain its dividend payments.

The dividend payout ratio measures the percentage of earnings a company distributes as dividends. It is calculated by dividing total dividend payments by net income. A lower payout ratio suggests that a company retains more earnings for reinvestment, while a higher ratio indicates that a larger portion of profits is distributed to shareholders. Companies with excessively high payout ratios may struggle to sustain dividend payments during economic downturns.

Investors looking for stable dividend stocks often seek companies with moderate payout ratios and a history of consistent dividend increases. Dividend growth stocks, such as those in the Dividend Aristocrats category, have increased their dividends annually for at least 25 consecutive years, signaling long-term financial strength and shareholder commitment.

Stock Splits

A stock split is a corporate action that increases the number of outstanding shares while proportionally reducing the stock price. Stock splits do not affect a company's market capitalization or total shareholder value but are used to make shares more affordable and attractive to investors. Companies typically split their stock when the price has risen significantly, making it less accessible to small investors.

In a 2-for-1 stock split, each shareholder receives an additional share for every share they own, and the stock price is cut in half.

For example, if a company's stock is trading at $200 per share and undergoes a 2-for-1 split, shareholders will now own twice as many shares, but each will be worth $100. The overall investment value remains the same, but the increased share count can lead to greater trading liquidity and investor participation.

Stock splits are often viewed as a positive signal in the market, as they indicate that a company's stock price has appreciated significantly. Investors may perceive a stock split as a sign of company growth and increased future earnings potential. However, stock splits do not change the fundamental value of a company, and long-term investors should focus on underlying business performance rather than stock price adjustments.

Reverse Stock Splits

Unlike regular stock splits that increase the number of shares, a reverse stock split reduces the number of outstanding shares while increasing the stock price. A company may conduct a reverse split to boost its stock price and meet exchange listing requirements. For example, in a 1-for-5 reverse stock split, five existing shares are consolidated into one, and the stock price increases fivefold.

Reverse stock splits are generally viewed as negative because they often occur when a company's stock price has fallen significantly. Struggling companies may use reverse splits to prevent delisting from major exchanges, but they do not address the underlying financial issues affecting the company's performance.

CHAPTER 4
DEBT SECURITIES

BONDS AND THEIR CHARACTERISTICS

Bonds are fixed-income securities issued by governments, corporations, municipalities, and other organizations to finance projects and operations. When an investor purchases a bond, they are essentially lending money to the issuer for a specified period. In exchange, the issuer agrees to pay periodic interest payments, known as coupon payments, and return the principal amount (face value) at maturity. Bonds are considered fixed-income investments because they provide regular interest payments over their lifetime.

Bonds are popular among investors who seek stable returns, lower risk compared to stocks, and predictable income streams. Unlike stocks, which fluctuate in value based on market performance and company earnings, bonds offer fixed payments that make them an attractive choice for conservative investors, retirees, and those looking to preserve capital.

Face Value (Par Value)

The face value or par value of a bond is the amount that the investor will receive when the bond matures. It is the principal amount that the issuer agrees to repay at the end of the bond's term. Most bonds have a standard face value of $1,000 per bond, though larger or institutional bonds may have higher denominations.

The face value is important because it determines the interest payments an investor receives. For example, if a bond has a 5% coupon rate and a face value of $1,000, the investor will receive $50 in interest per year ($1,000 × 5%). Even if the bond trades at a different market price, the interest payments are always calculated based on the face value.

Coupon Rate and Interest Payments

The coupon rate of a bond represents the fixed interest rate that the issuer agrees to pay bondholders over the bond's lifetime. The rate is expressed as a percentage of the bond's face value and determines how much income an investor will receive annually.

For example, if a corporate bond has a 6% coupon rate and a face value of $1,000, the investor will receive $60 per year in interest payments. The coupon payments are typically made semi-annually, meaning the investor would receive $30 every six months.

The coupon rate is fixed at the time of issuance and does not change over the bond's life. However, bondholders may choose to sell their bonds in the secondary market before maturity, where bond prices fluctuate based on interest rate movements, issuer credit quality, and market demand.

Bonds with higher coupon rates are generally more attractive to investors, as they provide higher income. However, the coupon rate is directly influenced by the issuer's creditworthiness, prevailing interest rates, and overall economic conditions.

Maturity Date

The maturity date of a bond is the date on which the issuer repays the principal amount (face value) to the bondholder. Bonds have different maturities, ranging from short-term (less than three years), medium-term (three to ten years), and long-term (more than ten years).

Short-term bonds tend to have lower yields but are considered less risky since the issuer's ability to repay the debt is more predictable. Long-term bonds usually offer higher interest rates but come with greater risk, as market conditions and interest rates can fluctuate significantly over extended periods.

Investors typically choose bond maturities based on their investment goals, risk tolerance, and market outlook. Those seeking capital preservation and stability may prefer short-term bonds, while investors looking for higher yields and income growth may opt for long-term bonds.

Bond Ratings and Credit Risk

Credit risk is a major factor in bond investing, as it measures the issuer's ability to meet interest and principal payments. Bonds are assigned credit ratings by agencies such as Moody's, Standard & Poor's (S&P), and Fitch, which assess the issuer's financial health and likelihood of default.

Investment-grade bonds, such as those rated AAA, AA, A, or BBB, are considered low-risk and suitable for conservative investors.

These bonds are issued by financially stable entities with a strong ability to meet debt obligations.

High-yield or junk bonds are rated BB or lower and carry greater risk of default. These bonds offer higher interest rates to compensate for their increased risk. While high-yield bonds can provide attractive returns, they are more susceptible to economic downturns and market volatility.

Investors must evaluate credit ratings, financial performance, and economic conditions before investing in bonds to ensure they align with their risk tolerance and investment objectives.

Market Price and Yield

Bonds trade in the secondary market, where their prices fluctuate based on interest rates, credit risk, and investor demand. A bond's market price may be different from its face value, leading to bonds being sold at a premium (above face value) or discount (below face value).

When interest rates rise, bond prices generally fall, as newly issued bonds offer higher yields. Conversely, when interest rates decline, bond prices increase, as existing bonds with higher coupon rates become more attractive.

The yield to maturity (YTM) represents the total return an investor can expect if they hold the bond until it matures. It considers the bond's current market price, coupon payments, and time to maturity, providing a more accurate measure of investment returns than the coupon rate alone.

CORPORATE, MUNICIPAL, AND GOVERNMENT BONDS

Bonds are a crucial component of the financial markets, serving as a means for governments, municipalities, and corporations to raise capital. Unlike equity securities, which provide ownership in a company, bonds represent a loan agreement between the issuer and the investor. Bondholders lend money to the issuing entity in exchange for periodic interest payments and the repayment of the principal amount at maturity. The three main categories of bonds—corporate bonds, municipal bonds, and government bonds—differ based on their issuers, risk levels, tax advantages, and return potential. Understanding the characteristics of each type of bond is essential for investors seeking stable income, portfolio diversification, and risk-adjusted returns.

Corporate Bonds

Corporate bonds are debt instruments issued by companies to raise capital for various business activities, such as product development, acquisitions, and refinancing existing debt. When an investor buys a corporate bond, they are lending money to the company, which agrees to pay interest (coupon payments) periodically and return the principal at maturity. Corporate bonds offer higher yields than government and municipal bonds due to the additional risk associated with lending to private enterprises.

Companies issue corporate bonds to secure funding without diluting ownership. Unlike issuing new shares of stock, which dilutes shareholder equity, issuing bonds allows companies to raise capital while maintaining control over their business operations. Corporate bonds are classified based on their credit quality, maturity, and structure.

The creditworthiness of a corporate bond issuer is a key factor in determining its risk level and interest rate. Credit rating agencies such as Moody's, Standard & Poor's (S&P), and Fitch assign ratings to corporate bonds, evaluating the company's ability to meet its debt obligations. Bonds rated AAA to BBB are considered investment-grade bonds, indicating lower risk, while bonds rated BB or lower are classified as high-yield (junk) bonds, which offer higher returns to compensate for the greater risk of default.

Corporate bonds can have different maturity periods, including short-term (less than three years), medium-term (three to ten years), and long-term (more than ten years). Longer-term corporate bonds generally offer higher yields to compensate for the increased uncertainty over extended periods.

One of the key advantages of corporate bonds is their higher interest rates compared to government bonds. Since corporations are subject to business risks such as competition, economic downturns, and industry disruptions, investors demand higher returns to compensate for the added risk. Corporate bonds are particularly attractive to income-focused investors looking for stable returns that exceed those of government securities.

Corporate bonds also offer a wide range of structures, including convertible bonds, callable bonds, and floating-rate bonds. Convertible bonds give investors the option to convert their bonds into company stock under specific conditions, offering potential equity upside. Callable bonds allow the issuer to redeem the bond before its maturity date, typically when interest rates decline, so they can refinance at lower rates. Floating-rate bonds have interest rates that adjust periodically based on market benchmarks, providing protection against rising rates.

Despite their benefits, corporate bonds carry default risk, meaning that if a company faces financial difficulties, it may be unable to make interest payments or repay principal at maturity. Investors mitigate this risk by diversifying across different corporate issuers and sectors, ensuring that a single default does not significantly impact their portfolio.

Municipal Bonds

Municipal bonds, also known as munis, are debt securities issued by state, county, and local governments to fund public projects such as highways, schools, water systems, and public transportation. These bonds provide investors with a steady income stream and tax advantages, making them a preferred investment for individuals seeking tax-efficient returns.

One of the key benefits of municipal bonds is their tax-exempt status. Interest income earned from most municipal bonds is exempt from federal income tax, and in many cases, state and local taxes as well. This makes municipal bonds particularly attractive to high-income investors, as the tax savings can enhance overall investment returns.

Municipal bonds are generally classified into two main categories: general obligation (GO) bonds and revenue bonds.

General obligation (GO) bonds are backed by the full faith and credit of the issuing municipality, meaning that the government entity pledges its general tax revenues to repay bondholders. These bonds are considered lower risk because they are supported by the government's ability to levy taxes. If necessary, municipalities can increase taxes to meet debt obligations.

Revenue bonds, in contrast, are backed by the revenue generated from a specific project or service. Examples include toll roads, airports, and water treatment facilities, where bond payments are funded by user fees and service charges rather than tax revenues. Since revenue bonds depend on the success of the project, they carry higher risk than general obligation bonds. Investors evaluate revenue bonds by assessing the project's financial feasibility, revenue projections, and operational efficiency.

Municipal bonds can have maturities ranging from short-term (one to three years) to long-term (20 to 30 years). Long-term munis tend to offer higher yields to compensate for the uncertainty over extended periods. However, since municipal bonds are typically low-risk investments, their yields are lower than those of corporate bonds.

While municipal bonds are considered safe investments, they are not completely risk-free. If a local government faces financial distress, budget deficits, or declining tax revenue, there is a risk of default. Credit rating agencies assign ratings to municipal bonds, helping investors assess their risk level before investing. Historically, municipal bond defaults have been rare, but they can occur in cases of extreme financial hardship.

Government Bonds

Government bonds are debt securities issued by national governments to fund public spending, infrastructure projects, and budget deficits. These bonds are considered the safest type of fixed-income investment, as they are backed by the full faith and credit of the issuing government. Since governments have the power to tax and print money, they are highly unlikely to default on their debt obligations.

In the United States, the most common government bonds are Treasury securities, which include Treasury bonds, Treasury notes, and Treasury bills (T-bills).

Treasury bonds (T-bonds) are long-term securities with maturities of 20 to 30 years. They provide fixed interest payments every six months and are favored by investors seeking long-term income stability. T-bonds offer lower yields than corporate bonds but are considered risk-free investments due to their government backing.

Treasury notes (T-notes) have maturities ranging from two to ten years and also pay interest semi-annually. These are popular among medium-term investors who want government-backed security with moderate returns.

Treasury bills (T-bills) are short-term securities with maturities ranging from a few days to one year. Unlike T-bonds and T-notes, T-bills do not pay periodic interest. Instead, they are issued at a discount to their face value and redeemed at full value upon maturity, with the difference representing the investor's return.

One of the key advantages of government bonds is their liquidity. U.S. Treasury securities are actively traded in the secondary market, allowing investors to buy and sell them easily.

Additionally, Treasuries are exempt from state and local taxes, further enhancing their appeal.

Government bonds play a crucial role in portfolio diversification, as they provide a hedge against stock market volatility. In times of economic uncertainty, investors often shift capital into Treasuries, driving prices higher and yields lower.

While government bonds are low risk, they are still subject to interest rate risk. When interest rates rise, bond prices fall, leading to potential losses for investors holding older, lower-yield bonds. However, investors can mitigate this risk by holding bonds to maturity or diversifying across different maturity periods.

Corporate, municipal, and government bonds each offer unique advantages and risks. Corporate bonds provide higher yields but carry default risk. Municipal bonds offer tax advantages and support public projects, making them attractive to income-seeking investors. Government bonds, particularly U.S. Treasuries, are the safest investments, providing stability and liquidity. Investors should carefully assess their risk tolerance, return expectations, and investment goals when choosing among these fixed-income securities.

BOND PRICING, YIELDS, AND INTEREST RATES

Bond Pricing

Bond pricing is determined by the present value of its future cash flows, which include periodic interest payments, known as coupon payments, and the final repayment of the bond's face value at maturity. Unlike stocks, which fluctuate based on market sentiment and company performance, bond prices are primarily influenced by interest rate movements, creditworthiness, and time to maturity. Since bonds offer fixed payments over their lifetime, their value in the secondary market changes in response to shifts in prevailing interest rates and risk factors.

When a bond is issued, it typically has a face value of $1,000, which represents the amount that will be repaid to the bondholder at maturity. However, once a bond begins trading in the secondary market, its price may differ from its face value. If market interest rates rise after the bond has been issued, newer bonds will be issued with higher coupon rates, making existing bonds with lower coupon rates less attractive. As a result, the price of older bonds will fall, allowing them to provide a comparable yield to newer, higher-yielding bonds. Conversely, if interest rates decline, previously issued bonds with higher coupon rates become more attractive, leading to an increase in their price. This inverse relationship between bond prices and interest rates is one of the most fundamental principles of fixed-income investing.

In addition to interest rate movements, bond prices are influenced by the credit quality of the issuer. Bonds issued by financially stable governments or corporations with strong credit ratings are generally considered lower risk and tend to trade at higher prices. In contrast, bonds issued by entities with weaker credit ratings must offer higher yields to attract investors, which results in lower market prices. Credit rating agencies such as Moody's, Standard & Poor's (S&P), and Fitch evaluate the creditworthiness of bond issuers and assign ratings that reflect the likelihood of default. Investment-grade bonds, which have high credit ratings, trade at higher prices due to their perceived safety, while lower-rated bonds, often referred to as junk bonds, trade at lower prices to compensate investors for the additional risk.

Bonds with longer maturities are generally more sensitive to interest rate changes than those with shorter maturities. This sensitivity is measured by a concept called duration, which quantifies the degree to which a bond's price will change in response to interest rate fluctuations. Long-term bonds tend to experience greater price swings when interest rates change because their fixed coupon payments are locked in for a longer period. As a result, investors seeking to minimize interest rate risk may prefer shorter-term bonds, which are less affected by market rate fluctuations.

Bond prices are also influenced by supply and demand dynamics in the market. When demand for bonds is high, prices tend to rise, and when demand weakens, prices decline. Investor sentiment, macroeconomic trends, and Federal Reserve policies all play a role in shaping demand for bonds. For example, during periods of economic uncertainty or stock market volatility, investors often seek the relative safety of bonds, driving prices higher. Conversely, when the economy is strong and interest rates are expected to rise, bond prices may decline as investors shift their focus to higher-yielding investments.

Understanding bond pricing requires an appreciation of the time value of money. Since bonds provide fixed cash flows over time, their market price is determined by discounting these future payments to their present value using the current market interest rate. The formula for bond pricing incorporates the present value of the coupon payments and the present value of the face value that will be received at maturity. This method ensures that bond investors receive a return that aligns with prevailing market conditions.

Bond Yields

Bond yields represent the return that an investor can expect to earn from holding a bond. Since bond prices fluctuate in the secondary market, yields provide a more accurate measure of return than the bond's stated coupon rate. There are several types of bond yields, each offering a different perspective on the bond's return potential.

The nominal yield, also known as the coupon yield, is the fixed interest rate stated on the bond when it is issued. This yield is calculated by dividing the annual coupon payment by the bond's face value. For example, if a bond has a face value of $1,000 and pays an annual coupon of $60, the nominal yield is 6%. This yield remains constant throughout the bond's life but does not account for changes in the bond's market price.

The current yield measures the bond's return based on its current market price rather than its face value. It is calculated by dividing the annual coupon payment by the bond's current market price. For example, if a bond has a coupon payment of $50 but is trading at $900, the current yield would be 5.56%. If the same bond were trading at a premium of $1,100, the current yield would drop to 4.54%. Current yield helps investors assess the income return on a bond relative to its market price but does not account for capital gains or losses if the bond is held until maturity.

The most comprehensive measure of a bond's return is the yield to maturity, which calculates the total return an investor will earn if they hold the bond until its maturity date. Yield to maturity takes into account the bond's coupon payments, the difference between its market price and face value, and the time remaining until maturity. This yield is useful for comparing bonds with different prices, coupon rates, and maturities, as it provides a standardized measure of return. If a bond is purchased at par, its yield to maturity equals its coupon rate. If purchased at a discount, its yield to maturity will be higher than the coupon rate, and if purchased at a premium, its yield to maturity will be lower than the coupon rate.

Some bonds, known as callable bonds, allow issuers to redeem them before maturity at a predetermined price. Yield to call measures the return an investor will receive if the bond is called before its scheduled maturity date. Callable bonds typically offer higher yields to compensate investors for the risk that the bond may be redeemed early, forcing them to reinvest at lower interest rates.

Another important measure is the yield spread, which compares the yield of a bond to a benchmark interest rate, such as U.S. Treasury yields. The yield spread reflects the level of risk associated with a bond relative to government securities, which are considered risk-free. A wider yield spread indicates higher perceived risk, while a narrower spread suggests lower risk.

Interest Rates

Interest rates play a crucial role in bond investing, as they have a direct impact on bond prices, yields, and overall market conditions. The relationship between bond prices and interest rates is inverse: when interest rates rise, bond prices fall, and when interest rates decline, bond prices increase. This occurs because new bonds issued in a higher interest rate environment offer better returns, making existing bonds with lower coupon rates less attractive. Investors will only buy older, lower-yielding bonds if their prices are reduced to compensate for the lower interest payments they provide.

Conversely, when interest rates fall, new bonds offer lower coupon rates, making previously issued bonds with higher fixed rates more desirable. This drives up the market prices of existing bonds, allowing investors who hold them to realize capital gains if they sell before maturity.

Interest rates are influenced by several factors, including monetary policy, inflation, and economic conditions. Central banks, such as the U.S. Federal Reserve, adjust interest rates to control inflation and economic growth. When the economy is growing too quickly, the Federal Reserve may raise interest rates to prevent inflation from rising too high. This makes borrowing more expensive, slows down economic activity, and causes bond prices to fall. On the other hand, during economic downturns, the Federal Reserve may lower interest rates to stimulate borrowing and investment, leading to higher bond prices.

Inflation also affects interest rates and bond yields. When inflation rises, the purchasing power of fixed bond payments declines, making bonds less attractive to investors. To compensate for inflation risk, bond yields must rise, which leads to a decline in bond prices. Investors closely monitor inflation trends and interest rate policies to anticipate changes in bond market conditions.

Market expectations also play a role in interest rate movements. If investors believe that interest rates will rise in the future, they may demand higher yields on bonds today, causing bond prices to fall. Similarly, if investors expect interest rates to decline, they may be willing to accept lower yields, leading to higher bond prices.

Understanding the dynamics of bond pricing, yields, and interest rates is crucial for fixed-income investors seeking to optimize returns while managing risk. By carefully analyzing these factors, investors can make informed decisions about bond selection, portfolio diversification, and interest rate exposure.

CHAPTER 5
OPTIONS

CALL AND PUT OPTIONS

Options are financial derivatives that provide investors with the right, but not the obligation, to buy or sell an underlying asset at a specified price before or at the expiration date. They are widely used in trading and investment strategies to hedge risk, generate income, or speculate on market movements. Options are categorized into two main types: call options and put options. Understanding these two options and how they function is essential for traders and investors looking to incorporate options into their portfolios.

A call option gives the holder the right to buy an underlying asset at a predetermined price, known as the strike price, within a specified period. Investors typically buy call options when they anticipate that the price of the underlying asset, such as a stock, will rise before the option's expiration. By using a call option, traders can benefit from the asset's price appreciation without committing the full amount required to buy the asset outright.

A put option gives the holder the right to sell an underlying asset at a predetermined strike price within a specified period.

Investors typically buy put options when they expect the price of the underlying asset to decline. Put options provide traders with a way to profit from falling markets or hedge against potential losses in their investment portfolios.

Options are traded on exchanges, such as the Chicago Board Options Exchange (CBOE), and derive their value from underlying assets, which can include stocks, indices, commodities, or currencies. Unlike stocks, which represent ownership in a company, options are contracts that expire after a fixed period, making them time-sensitive investments. The expiration period for an option can range from a few days to several months or even years, depending on the contract type.

Call Options

A call option provides the holder with the right to buy an underlying asset at a specific price within a set timeframe. The buyer of a call option expects the asset's price to increase, allowing them to buy the asset at a lower price and potentially sell it at a profit.

Each call option contract typically represents 100 shares of the underlying stock. For example, if an investor purchases one call option on a stock, they have the right to buy 100 shares of that stock at the strike price before the option expires.

The price of a call option, known as the premium, is determined by several factors, including the underlying asset's price, time to expiration, volatility, and interest rates. When the underlying asset's price rises, the value of a call option generally increases, as the likelihood of profiting from the option improves.

Call options can be used for various strategies, including speculation, hedging, and income generation. Traders who anticipate a stock will rise can buy call options to gain leveraged exposure without purchasing the stock outright. Investors who already own a stock can sell covered calls to generate income while limiting their upside potential. Institutions and hedge funds use call options as part of complex trading strategies to manage risk and optimize returns.

There are three key scenarios for call option holders:

In-the-Money (ITM):
A call option is in-the-money when the underlying asset's price is above the strike price. This means the option has intrinsic value and can be exercised for a profit.

At-the-Money (ATM):
A call option is at-the-money when the underlying asset's price is equal to the strike price. At this point, the option has no intrinsic value but may still have time value.

Out-of-the-Money (OTM):
A call option is out-of-the-money when the underlying asset's price is below the strike price. In this case, the option has no intrinsic value, and if it remains out-of-the-money until expiration, it will expire worthless.

For example, suppose an investor buys a call option on a stock with a strike price of $50 and an expiration date one month away. If the stock's price rises to $60, the investor can exercise the option and buy the stock at $50 per share, making a profit. If the stock price remains below $50, the option expires worthless, and the investor only loses the premium paid for the option.

Put Options

A put option gives the holder the right to sell an underlying asset at a specific price within a set timeframe. Investors typically buy put options when they expect the asset's price to decline, allowing them to sell at a higher price and potentially profit from the asset's depreciation.

Like call options, put option contracts also represent 100 shares of the underlying stock. If an investor buys one put option, they have the right to sell 100 shares of that stock at the strike price before expiration.

The price of a put option, or the premium, is influenced by the same factors as call options: the underlying asset's price, time until expiration, volatility, and interest rates. Put options increase in value when the underlying asset's price declines, as the likelihood of profiting from the option rises.

Put options are commonly used for hedging, speculation, and portfolio protection. Traders use put options to profit from stock declines, while long-term investors use them to hedge against potential market downturns. For instance, if an investor holds a large stock portfolio but fears a market decline, they can buy put options on major stock indices to limit losses.

There are three key scenarios for put option holders:

In-the-Money (ITM):
A put option is in-the-money when the underlying asset's price is below the strike price. This means the option has intrinsic value and can be exercised profitably.

At-the-Money (ATM):
A put option is at-the-money when the underlying asset's price is equal to the strike price. It has no intrinsic value but retains time value.

Out-of-the-Money (OTM):
A put option is out-of-the-money when the underlying asset's price is above the strike price. It has no intrinsic value and will expire worthless if the price remains unchanged.

For example, suppose an investor buys a put option on a stock with a strike price of $50 and an expiration date one month away. If the stock price drops to $40, the investor can exercise the option and sell the stock at $50 per share, making a profit. If the stock price stays above $50, the option expires worthless, and the investor loses only the premium paid for the option.

Key Differences Between Call and Put Options

Call and put options serve opposite purposes in the market. Call options are used to profit from rising stock prices, while put options are used to profit from falling stock prices. Investors buy call options when they expect an increase in the price of the underlying asset and buy put options when they anticipate a decline.

The risk and reward structures for call and put options differ as well. When buying a call option, the maximum loss is limited to the premium paid, while the potential profit is unlimited if the stock price rises significantly. When buying a put option, the maximum loss is also limited to the premium paid, while the maximum profit is limited to the stock's price falling to zero.

Traders also use options for income generation. Selling covered call options allows investors to collect premiums in exchange for agreeing to sell their shares at a predetermined price. Selling cash-secured put options enables investors to collect premiums while committing to buy shares at a set price if the option is exercised.

OPTION STRATEGIES AND RISKS

Options trading offers a variety of strategies that cater to different market conditions and investment objectives. These strategies can be used for speculation, hedging, or income generation while managing risks effectively. Unlike stock trading, where investors buy or sell shares outright, options allow traders to control larger positions with less capital. However, options also carry unique risks, and choosing the right strategy depends on factors such as market outlook, volatility, time horizon, and risk tolerance.

There are three broad categories of option strategies: basic strategies, which involve a single option contract; intermediate strategies, which combine multiple options for risk management; and advanced strategies, which involve complex multi-leg positions designed to optimize risk and reward.

Basic Option Strategies

Long Call Strategy

The long call strategy is used when a trader expects the price of a stock or underlying asset to rise. A call option gives the trader the right to buy the asset at a specified strike price before the expiration date.

The primary advantage of a long call is leverage, as it allows an investor to control a large number of shares without purchasing them outright. However, options have an expiration date, meaning the trade must move in the desired direction within a certain timeframe.

The maximum loss is limited to the premium paid for the call option, while the potential profit is unlimited, as the stock price can continue to rise indefinitely. If the stock price does not increase above the strike price before expiration, the option becomes worthless, and the investor loses the premium.

Long Put Strategy

A long put strategy is used when a trader expects a stock's price to decline. A put option gives the trader the right to sell the asset at a specified price before expiration.

This strategy benefits from downward price movements, making it an effective way to hedge a long stock position or speculate on bearish trends. If the stock price falls below the strike price, the trader can sell the asset at a higher price and potentially make a profit.

The maximum loss is the premium paid for the put option, while the maximum profit occurs if the stock's price drops to zero. If the stock price remains above the strike price, the option expires worthless, and the trader loses the premium.

Covered Call Strategy

A covered call strategy is used by investors who own shares of a stock and want to generate additional income by selling call options against their holdings. The goal is to collect the premium from selling the call option while limiting the potential upside of the stock.

If the stock price stays below the strike price, the call option expires worthless, and the investor keeps both the stock and the premium. If the stock price rises above the strike price, the investor must sell the stock at the agreed-upon price, potentially missing out on additional gains.

Covered calls are considered a low-risk strategy, but they cap the potential upside of the stock. This strategy works well for investors looking to earn passive income while holding long-term stock positions.

Cash-Secured Put Strategy

The cash-secured put strategy involves selling a put option while setting aside enough cash to buy the stock if the option is exercised. Investors use this strategy when they want to acquire shares at a lower price while collecting income from the premium.

If the stock price stays above the strike price, the put option expires worthless, and the trader keeps the premium as profit. If the stock price falls below the strike price, the investor is obligated to buy the stock at the agreed-upon price.

This strategy is ideal for investors who want to buy stocks at a discount while earning extra income. However, there is a risk of the stock price falling significantly, leading to losses if the investor is forced to buy at a higher strike price than the market value.

Intermediate Option Strategies

Bull Call Spread

A bull call spread is a strategy used when an investor expects a moderate increase in a stock's price. It involves buying a call option at a lower strike price and selling a call option at a higher strike price with the same expiration date.

The benefit of a bull call spread is that it reduces the cost of entering the trade compared to buying a single call option. However, the profit is capped at the difference between the strike prices, limiting the maximum potential return.

This strategy provides a balanced risk-reward profile, making it suitable for traders looking to take advantage of modest price movements while managing their downside risk.

Bear Put Spread

A bear put spread is a bearish strategy that involves buying a put option at a higher strike price and selling a put option at a lower strike price with the same expiration date.

The goal of this strategy is to profit from a decline in the underlying stock's price while reducing the cost of buying a put option. The trade-off is that potential gains are capped at the difference between the two strike prices.

Bear put spreads are often used when traders expect a moderate decline in stock prices rather than a major selloff.

Iron Condor Strategy

The iron condor is a non-directional strategy used when a trader expects a stock to remain within a certain range. It involves selling a bull put spread and a bear call spread simultaneously, creating a profit zone between the two spreads.

If the stock price remains within the range, both options expire worthless, and the trader keeps the premium collected. If the stock price moves beyond the range, losses occur.

This strategy works best in low-volatility markets, where stock prices tend to trade within a narrow range. It allows traders to collect consistent premium income while limiting potential risks.

Advanced Option Strategies

Straddle Strategy

A straddle strategy involves buying both a call and a put option with the same strike price and expiration date. This strategy profits from large price movements in either direction.

If the stock moves significantly up or down, one of the options will gain enough value to cover the loss on the other option and generate a profit. If the stock price remains stable, both options may expire worthless, leading to a loss equal to the premium paid.

Straddles are often used ahead of earnings reports, economic data releases, or major company announcements, where significant volatility is expected.

Strangle Strategy

A strangle strategy is similar to a straddle but involves buying a call and a put option at different strike prices. This reduces the cost compared to a straddle but requires a larger price movement to be profitable.

If the stock moves significantly up or down, one of the options will become profitable. However, if the stock remains within the range, both options expire worthless, resulting in a total loss of the premium paid.

Strangles are used when traders expect volatility but are uncertain about the direction of the move.

THE OPTIONS CLEARING CORPORATION (OCC)

The Options Clearing Corporation (OCC) is the primary clearinghouse for equity options and other derivative products in the United States. Established in 1973, the OCC plays a crucial role in the financial markets by ensuring the smooth execution, clearing, and settlement of options transactions. It provides stability and security to the options market by acting as a central counterparty (CCP) for trades, guaranteeing that both buyers and sellers fulfill their contractual obligations.

As an industry leader, the OCC is regulated by several federal agencies, including the Securities and Exchange Commission (SEC), the Commodity Futures Trading Commission (CFTC), and the Board of Governors of the Federal Reserve System. These regulatory bodies oversee the OCC's operations to ensure it maintains financial integrity, market transparency, and compliance with legal requirements.

The OCC's role extends beyond simple trade clearing. It actively manages risk, enforces margin requirements, and protects market participants from counterparty default. By serving as a neutral intermediary between buyers and sellers, the OCC ensures that traders, brokerage firms, and institutional investors can engage in options trading with confidence.

Role of the OCC in the Options Market

The OCC serves as the backbone of the options market, providing security and efficiency in trade execution and settlement. Its core responsibilities include clearing trades, managing risk, and enforcing financial regulations.

One of the most important functions of the OCC is acting as a guarantor for every options contract traded on regulated exchanges such as the Chicago Board Options Exchange (CBOE), Nasdaq, and NYSE American Options. When a trader buys or sells an option, they do not transact directly with another trader. Instead, the OCC becomes the counterparty to both sides of the trade, ensuring that the transaction is executed and honored regardless of the financial condition of the original buyer or seller.

Clearing trades through the OCC eliminates counterparty risk, meaning that traders do not have to worry about the other party defaulting on their obligations. This system enhances the liquidity and stability of the options market by allowing traders to buy and sell contracts without fear of financial loss due to non-performance.

The OCC also facilitates the exercise and assignment of options contracts. When an option holder decides to exercise their contract, the OCC ensures that the correct amount of shares or cash is delivered to fulfill the contract's terms. Similarly, if an option is assigned, the OCC randomly selects an option seller to meet the contract's obligations. This process maintains fairness and prevents manipulation in the options market.

Trade Clearing and Settlement Process

The OCC follows a structured process for clearing and settling options transactions, ensuring that all trades are properly recorded, confirmed, and executed.

When an options trade occurs on an exchange, the trade details are sent to the OCC for verification and processing. The OCC reviews the transaction to ensure it meets all compliance and risk management standards. Once verified, the OCC becomes the counterparty to both the buyer and the seller, guaranteeing that the contract will be honored.

Each day, the OCC issues settlement instructions to clearing firms and brokers, detailing the transactions that must be settled. If an option is exercised, the OCC ensures that shares of the underlying asset are transferred from the assigned seller to the exercising buyer. If an option expires worthless, the contract is simply removed from the trader's account, and no further action is needed.

This automated and regulated process ensures that all market participants fulfill their obligations efficiently and without delays. By centralizing clearing operations, the OCC minimizes the risk of failed trades, enhances liquidity, and promotes market confidence.

Margin Requirements and Risk Management

Risk management is a critical component of the OCC's operations. Because options trading involves leverage and financial obligations, the OCC enforces margin requirements to protect against default and systemic risk.

When traders sell (write) options, they assume an obligation to fulfill the contract's terms if assigned. To ensure they can meet these obligations, the OCC requires traders to maintain sufficient collateral in their brokerage accounts. This collateral, known as margin, acts as a financial safeguard against potential losses.

The OCC calculates margin requirements based on the Options Price Reporting Authority (OPRA) volatility models, historical price movements, and market conditions. The amount of margin required depends on factors such as the strike price, expiration date, and market volatility of the underlying asset. Higher volatility results in higher margin requirements because the risk of significant price swings is greater.

In extreme market conditions, the OCC has the authority to adjust margin requirements and take additional risk control measures. This flexibility helps maintain financial stability and prevents widespread defaults that could disrupt the broader financial system.

Clearing firms, which act as intermediaries between the OCC and traders, are also required to meet strict capital requirements to ensure they can support their customers' trading activities. If a clearing firm fails to meet its obligations, the OCC can liquidate its positions and use its financial reserves to prevent losses from spreading throughout the market.

Options Exercise and Assignment Process

The OCC oversees the exercise and assignment of options contracts, ensuring a fair and systematic process for all market participants.

When an option holder chooses to exercise their contract, they notify their broker, who then submits the request to the OCC. The OCC processes the request and arranges for the appropriate shares or cash to be transferred from the assigned seller to the exercising buyer.

For call options, this means the exercising trader buys the underlying asset at the strike price, while the assigned seller must deliver the shares at that price. For put options, the exercising trader sells the underlying asset, and the assigned seller must buy it at the strike price.

Assignment of an options contract is randomly determined by the OCC using a standardized selection process. This ensures that all traders who have written (sold) options have an equal chance of being assigned. Brokers receive assignment notifications from the OCC and distribute them to their clients accordingly.

To protect against sudden spikes in assignments, the OCC employs automated risk controls that prevent large-scale disruptions in the market. These controls ensure that assignments are managed in an orderly fashion and that traders have adequate time to respond.

Regulatory Oversight and Compliance

The OCC operates under the supervision of multiple regulatory agencies to maintain financial stability and market integrity. The SEC oversees the OCC's options-clearing operations, ensuring compliance with securities laws, while the CFTC regulates derivatives transactions to prevent fraud and market manipulation. The Federal Reserve provides additional oversight, ensuring that the OCC maintains adequate liquidity to support its clearing functions.

The OCC is required to maintain substantial financial reserves to cover potential defaults and market disruptions. It also conducts stress testing and scenario analysis to prepare for extreme market conditions. These tests help the OCC identify weaknesses in the financial system and implement safeguards before problems arise.

Clearing members, which include banks and brokerage firms, must meet strict capital requirements to participate in the OCC's clearing operations. These requirements help prevent systemic failures and ensure that clearing firms can support their clients' trading activities without defaulting.

To enhance transparency, the OCC regularly publishes financial reports, margin policy updates, and risk management assessments. These reports help market participants understand the OCC's role in maintaining stability and reducing risk in the options market.

Importance of the OCC in Financial Markets

The OCC plays a critical role in maintaining confidence and efficiency in the financial markets. By guaranteeing trade execution, managing risk, and enforcing financial regulations, the OCC ensures that options markets remain liquid and reliable.

Without the OCC, the options market would be far more vulnerable to counterparty risk, meaning that traders would have to worry about whether their counterparties could fulfill their obligations. This would lead to higher transaction costs, reduced liquidity, and increased uncertainty.

By acting as a central counterparty, the OCC eliminates these risks and allows traders to focus on executing their strategies without concerns about trade settlement. This system also helps attract institutional investors, hedge funds, and retail traders to the options market, further increasing liquidity and price efficiency.

CHAPTER 6

MUTUAL FUNDS AND INVESTMENT COMPANIES

TYPES OF MUTUAL FUNDS

Mutual funds are one of the most popular investment vehicles for individual and institutional investors seeking diversification, professional management, and access to a broad range of assets. A mutual fund is a pooled investment that collects money from multiple investors to purchase a diversified portfolio of stocks, bonds, or other securities. Managed by professional fund managers, mutual funds allow investors to participate in financial markets without directly managing individual securities.

Mutual funds are classified into different categories based on investment objectives, asset classes, and risk levels. Investors can choose from equity funds, bond funds, balanced funds, money market funds, index funds, sector funds, and international funds, among others. Each type of mutual fund is designed to meet specific investment goals, such as capital appreciation, income generation, or risk minimization.

Understanding the various types of mutual funds helps investors select funds that align with their financial goals, risk tolerance, and investment horizon.

Equity Mutual Funds

Equity mutual funds invest primarily in stocks and aim to provide long-term capital appreciation. These funds are best suited for investors with higher risk tolerance and a long investment horizon, as stock prices tend to be volatile in the short term but offer superior growth potential over time.

There are several subcategories of equity mutual funds, each focusing on different investment strategies:

Growth Funds focus on stocks of companies with high growth potential. These companies may not pay dividends but reinvest their earnings to expand operations. Growth funds tend to be more volatile but offer higher long-term return potential.

Value Funds invest in undervalued stocks that are trading at prices lower than their intrinsic worth. Fund managers identify companies with strong fundamentals but temporarily low stock prices, expecting them to appreciate over time. Value funds tend to be less volatile than growth funds and are suitable for long-term investors seeking steady returns.

Dividend Funds invest in companies that consistently pay dividends. These funds are ideal for investors seeking regular income in addition to capital appreciation. Dividend funds are often less volatile and can provide a cushion during market downturns.

Large-Cap, Mid-Cap, and Small-Cap Funds focus on companies based on their market capitalization. Large-cap funds invest in established, financially stable companies, offering lower risk but moderate growth. Mid-cap funds invest in medium-sized companies with higher growth potential but slightly more risk. Small-cap funds focus on smaller, fast-growing companies, providing the highest growth potential but also the highest volatility.

Sector Funds concentrate investments in specific industries, such as technology, healthcare, energy, or financial services. These funds allow investors to gain targeted exposure to high-growth sectors but come with higher risk due to their lack of diversification.

Index Funds track the performance of a stock market index, such as the S&P 500 or Nasdaq 100. These funds have low expense ratios and aim to mirror market performance rather than outperform it. Index funds are popular among passive investors who prefer a long-term, low-cost investment approach.

Bond Mutual Funds

Bond mutual funds invest in fixed-income securities, such as government bonds, corporate bonds, and municipal bonds. These funds are ideal for investors seeking regular income and lower volatility compared to equity funds.

Bond funds are classified based on the type of bonds they hold:

Government Bond Funds invest in bonds issued by national governments, such as U.S. Treasury bonds. These funds are considered low-risk investments because they are backed by the government.

Corporate Bond Funds invest in bonds issued by companies. These funds offer higher yields than government bond funds but carry more credit risk, as companies may default on their bond payments.

Municipal Bond Funds invest in bonds issued by state and local governments. The interest earned from municipal bonds is often tax-free, making these funds attractive to investors in higher tax brackets.

High-Yield Bond Funds (also known as junk bond funds) invest in lower-rated bonds that offer higher yields to compensate for the increased risk of default. These funds provide higher returns but carry significant credit risk.

Inflation-Protected Bond Funds invest in Treasury Inflation-Protected Securities (TIPS), which adjust for inflation. These funds help investors preserve purchasing power in inflationary environments.

Balanced Funds (Hybrid Funds)

Balanced funds, also known as hybrid funds, invest in a mix of stocks and bonds to provide both capital appreciation and income. These funds are designed to balance risk and reward, making them suitable for moderate-risk investors.

There are different types of balanced funds:

Aggressive Allocation Funds hold a higher percentage of stocks, typically 60-80% equities and 20-40% bonds, offering higher growth potential but also greater volatility.

Conservative Allocation Funds allocate more assets to bonds, typically 60-80% fixed income and 20-40% equities, prioritizing income and capital preservation over growth.

Target-Date Funds adjust their asset allocation based on a predetermined retirement date. These funds start with a higher allocation to stocks and gradually shift toward bonds and cash as the target date approaches, making them ideal for retirement planning.

Money Market Mutual Funds

Money market funds invest in short-term, low-risk securities, such as Treasury bills, commercial paper, and certificates of deposit (CDs). These funds provide liquidity, stability, and modest returns, making them ideal for investors who need a safe place to park cash while earning some interest.

Money market funds are often used as emergency funds or cash reserves because they offer high liquidity and principal protection. However, they provide lower returns compared to stock or bond funds.

International and Global Funds

International and global funds invest in stocks and bonds from foreign markets, offering exposure to global economic growth.

International Funds invest exclusively in foreign companies, excluding U.S.-based investments. These funds allow investors to diversify beyond the domestic market and capitalize on growth opportunities in emerging economies.

Global Funds invest in both U.S. and foreign companies, providing broad diversification across multiple markets.

Emerging Market Funds focus on developing economies, such as China, India, and Brazil, where growth potential is high but comes with increased volatility and currency risks.

Foreign Bond Funds invest in government and corporate bonds issued outside the U.S. These funds help investors diversify their fixed-income portfolios while gaining exposure to global interest rate trends.

Specialty Mutual Funds

Specialty mutual funds focus on unique investment strategies that do not fit traditional categories. These funds allow investors to target specific market trends, alternative assets, or ethical investing principles.

ESG (Environmental, Social, and Governance) Funds invest in companies that meet ethical, environmental, and social responsibility standards. These funds cater to socially conscious investors who want their investments to align with their values.

Real Estate Investment Trust (REIT) Funds invest in publicly traded real estate companies and provide exposure to the real estate sector without direct property ownership.

Commodity Funds invest in gold, oil, agricultural products, and other natural resources. These funds offer a hedge against inflation but come with higher volatility.

Hedge Fund Replication Funds mimic hedge fund strategies, such as long-short investing and market-neutral approaches, without the high fees and restrictions of traditional hedge funds.

FUND STRUCTURES AND FEES

Mutual funds are structured in various ways to accommodate different investor preferences, regulatory requirements, and investment strategies. Understanding fund structures helps investors choose the right type of mutual fund that aligns with their investment objectives, whether they seek capital appreciation, income generation, risk management, or liquidity.

Apart from their structure, mutual funds charge different fees that impact overall returns. These fees cover fund management, administrative costs, marketing expenses, and transaction costs. Some fees are transparent and upfront, while others are embedded in the expense ratio, making them less visible but equally important in assessing the total cost of ownership.

A mutual fund's structure and fees play a critical role in an investor's net returns, making it essential to analyze costs before investing. This chapter explores different fund structures, how they operate, and the fees associated with mutual fund investments.

Types of Mutual Fund Structures

Mutual funds are categorized based on how they issue and redeem shares, their trading mechanism, and how they are managed. The three primary fund structures include open-end funds, closed-end funds, and exchange-traded funds (ETFs). Each structure has unique features that impact liquidity, pricing, and investment strategy.

Open-End Funds

Open-end funds are the most common type of mutual fund. They do not have a fixed number of shares and continuously issue new shares to investors and redeem existing shares upon request. This means that the number of shares outstanding fluctuates based on investor demand.

Investors can buy and sell shares directly from the fund company at the net asset value (NAV), which is calculated at the end of each trading day based on the total market value of the fund's assets. Unlike stocks or ETFs, which trade throughout the day, open-end funds do not have intraday price movements.

Because open-end funds allow unlimited inflows and outflows, fund managers must maintain a portion of assets in cash to meet redemptions. This can affect investment performance, as the fund may not be fully invested in securities.

One of the benefits of open-end funds is high liquidity. Investors can enter or exit the fund at any time without worrying about market fluctuations affecting their ability to sell. However, because share transactions are based on NAV rather than market prices, investors may not know the exact price at which they are buying or selling until the market closes.

Closed-End Funds

Closed-end funds operate differently from open-end funds. They issue a fixed number of shares during an initial public offering (IPO), after which they trade on a stock exchange like regular stocks. Once the fund is launched, investors can only buy or sell shares on the secondary market, as the fund does not create new shares or redeem existing ones.

Since closed-end funds trade on an exchange, their market price is determined by supply and demand, rather than directly reflecting the NAV of the fund's assets. This means that closed-end fund shares can trade at a premium or discount to NAV. If demand for the fund is high, shares may trade at a premium, whereas low demand can cause shares to trade at a discount.

One advantage of closed-end funds is that they do not have to maintain cash reserves for redemptions, allowing fund managers to be fully invested in assets for potentially higher returns. However, because share prices fluctuate independently of NAV, closed-end funds can be more volatile than open-end funds.

Exchange-Traded Funds (ETFs)

ETFs are a hybrid between open-end and closed-end funds, offering the diversification of mutual funds and the trading flexibility of stocks. ETFs trade on stock exchanges throughout the day, allowing investors to buy and sell shares at market prices rather than at NAV.

Unlike closed-end funds, which have a fixed number of shares, ETFs use a creation and redemption mechanism involving authorized participants (APs). These APs create or redeem ETF shares based on investor demand, helping the ETF price stay close to its NAV.

ETFs have become increasingly popular due to their low expense ratios, tax efficiency, and intraday trading flexibility. Passive ETFs, which track an index like the S&P 500, have lower costs compared to actively managed mutual funds. However, actively managed ETFs do exist and may have higher fees.

Mutual Fund Share Classes

Mutual funds offer different share classes that determine how fees and expenses are charged. The most common share classes include Class A, Class B, and Class C shares, each with different fee structures and investment implications.

Class A Shares

Class A shares charge a front-end load, meaning investors pay a sales commission when purchasing shares. This fee is deducted upfront, reducing the initial investment amount.

For example, if an investor puts $10,000 into a Class A mutual fund with a 5% front-end load, they will only invest $9,500, as $500 goes toward the sales charge.

Although Class A shares require an upfront cost, they usually have lower annual expense ratios, making them a good choice for long-term investors. Some funds offer breakpoint discounts, where the sales charge decreases for larger investments.

Class B Shares

Class B shares do not have a front-end load but charge a contingent deferred sales charge (CDSC), also known as a back-end load. Investors pay this fee when selling shares within a certain period (typically 5-7 years).

The back-end load decreases over time and eventually disappears after a set number of years, at which point Class B shares may convert into Class A shares with lower annual expenses.

Although Class B shares offer the benefit of no upfront fees, they generally have higher annual expense ratios, which can erode long-term returns. They are best for medium-term investors who plan to hold the fund until the load disappears.

Class C Shares

Class C shares charge a level load, meaning they have no front-end or back-end sales charges but have higher ongoing expenses. Investors may face small redemption fees if they sell within the first year.

Due to their higher annual fees, Class C shares are best for short-term investors who do not plan to hold the fund for long periods. Over time, the higher expense ratio can make Class C shares more costly than Class A or Class B shares.

Mutual Fund Fees and Expenses

Mutual funds charge various fees to cover operational costs, fund management, and marketing. These fees impact overall returns and should be carefully analyzed before selecting a fund.

Expense Ratio

The expense ratio represents the total annual cost of running a mutual fund as a percentage of its total assets. It includes:

- Management Fees: Paid to professional fund managers who oversee the portfolio.
- Administrative Fees: Cover operational costs like recordkeeping and compliance.
- 12b-1 Fees: Marketing and distribution costs to promote the fund.

Lower expense ratios improve investment returns. Index funds and ETFs typically have lower expense ratios than actively managed funds.

Load Fees

Some mutual funds charge sales loads, which are commissions paid to financial advisors or brokers. These include:

- Front-end loads (Class A shares) – Paid at purchase.
- Back-end loads (Class B shares) – Paid at redemption.
- Level loads (Class C shares) – Ongoing costs.

Transaction Costs

Funds that frequently buy and sell securities incur trading costs, including brokerage fees and bid-ask spreads. Actively managed funds typically have higher trading costs than passive funds.

SUITABILITY FOR INVESTORS

Investment Objectives

Before investing in mutual funds, investors must clearly define their financial objectives. Mutual funds cater to various investment goals, whether it is long-term capital appreciation, generating income, or preserving capital. Investors seeking capital growth should focus on equity funds that provide higher returns over extended periods but come with greater risk. Those looking for income generation may prefer bond funds or dividend-paying stock funds that offer consistent returns. For investors prioritizing capital preservation, low-risk mutual funds such as money market funds or government bond funds provide stability and protection against market downturns. Understanding investment objectives helps in selecting the right fund that aligns with personal financial strategies.

Risk Tolerance

Risk tolerance varies among investors and plays a crucial role in determining the appropriate type of mutual fund. Some investors prefer stability and lower risk, while others are willing to endure market fluctuations for higher returns. Conservative investors typically opt for funds that minimize risk, such as government bond funds, municipal bond funds, and money market funds, which prioritize steady returns with minimal volatility. Moderate investors may be comfortable with a mix of stocks and bonds, selecting balanced funds or large-cap equity funds that offer growth potential while maintaining some level of risk control. Aggressive investors, who prioritize high returns over stability, often invest in small-cap funds, growth funds, or sector funds that have the potential for significant gains but also come with substantial volatility. Assessing risk tolerance ensures that investors select mutual funds that align with their ability to withstand market fluctuations.

Time Horizon

The length of time an investor plans to keep their money invested influences the choice of mutual funds. Investors with a long-term horizon, typically ten years or more, can afford to take on more risk and invest in equity funds that offer high growth potential. Market fluctuations tend to even out over long periods, allowing long-term investors to benefit from compounding returns. Investors with a medium-term horizon, ranging from five to ten years, may prefer balanced funds or bond funds that offer a mix of stability and growth. Those with a short-term horizon, looking to invest for fewer than five years, should focus on low-risk options such as money market funds or short-term bond funds that protect capital while providing modest returns. Matching mutual funds to the investment horizon helps investors manage risk and achieve their financial goals within the desired timeframe.

Liquidity Needs

Liquidity is an important factor when selecting a mutual fund, as it determines how quickly and easily an investor can access their money. Some funds, such as open-end mutual funds, allow investors to buy and sell shares at the net asset value on a daily basis, making them highly liquid. Money market funds and short-term bond funds also offer easy access to funds without significant price fluctuations. However, certain funds, such as closed-end funds, may have limited liquidity since they trade on stock exchanges, and their prices can fluctuate above or below net asset value. Mutual funds with exit loads or lock-in periods, such as tax-saving funds or retirement-focused funds, may restrict access to money for a specific period. Investors who require immediate access to their funds should choose liquid investment options, while those with a long-term perspective may prioritize higher returns over liquidity.

Diversification Preferences

Mutual funds provide diversification by investing in a broad range of securities, reducing the risk associated with holding a single asset. Some investors prefer actively managed funds that offer a well-diversified portfolio managed by professionals who adjust asset allocation based on market conditions. Others may prefer passively managed index funds that track the performance of a market index while maintaining low costs. Investors seeking global diversification may opt for international or emerging market funds that invest in foreign markets, spreading risk across different economies. Sector funds, on the other hand, concentrate investments in specific industries such as technology, healthcare, or energy, offering high growth potential but reduced diversification. Selecting mutual funds based on diversification preferences helps investors balance risk and return effectively.

Tax Considerations

Tax implications are an essential aspect of mutual fund suitability, as different funds have varying tax treatments. Investors looking for tax efficiency may prefer municipal bond funds, which offer tax-free interest income at the federal level and sometimes at the state level. Index funds and ETFs are also tax-efficient, as they have lower turnover and generate fewer taxable capital gains. Actively managed mutual funds, which frequently buy and sell securities, may result in higher taxable distributions, affecting after-tax returns. Retirement-focused funds, such as tax-advantaged accounts like IRAs or 401(k)s, allow investors to defer taxes on earnings until withdrawal. Tax-conscious investors should consider mutual funds that align with their tax planning strategies to maximize after-tax returns.

Income Requirements

Some investors rely on their investments for regular income, making income-generating mutual funds a suitable option. Bond funds, dividend equity funds, and real estate investment trust (REIT) funds provide periodic income in the form of interest or dividends. These funds are ideal for retirees or investors who need a steady cash flow while preserving capital. The frequency and stability of income distributions vary among funds, so investors must select funds that align with their financial needs. Growth-oriented investors, who do not require immediate income, may prefer funds that reinvest dividends and interest payments to maximize long-term wealth accumulation. Income-focused investors should evaluate mutual funds based on dividend yields, interest payments, and payout stability to ensure a reliable income stream.

Investment Costs and Fees

The cost of investing in mutual funds affects overall returns and should be considered when selecting a fund. Expense ratios, which include management fees, administrative costs, and marketing expenses, vary between actively managed and passively managed funds. Actively managed funds tend to have higher expense ratios due to frequent trading and professional management, while index funds and ETFs have lower costs, making them cost-effective choices for long-term investors. Some mutual funds charge sales loads, which are commissions paid when buying or selling shares, increasing investment costs. Investors should also be aware of 12b-1 fees, which cover marketing and distribution expenses, as they add to the fund's total costs. Choosing low-cost mutual funds can significantly impact long-term returns, making it essential for investors to evaluate fee structures before investing.

Inflation Protection

Investors concerned about inflation should consider mutual funds that offer protection against rising prices. Equity funds, particularly growth funds and small-cap funds, tend to outperform inflation over the long term by generating higher returns. Inflation-protected bond funds, such as Treasury Inflation-Protected Securities (TIPS) funds, provide a hedge against inflation by adjusting principal values based on inflation rates. Real asset funds, which invest in commodities, real estate, or infrastructure, can also serve as a safeguard against inflationary pressures. Fixed-income investors relying on bond income must be cautious, as inflation erodes the purchasing power of fixed payments. Selecting mutual funds with inflation protection features helps investors maintain their standard of living and purchasing power over time.

Market Conditions and Economic Environment

Market conditions and economic cycles influence mutual fund performance and should be considered when choosing an investment. During periods of economic expansion, equity funds, particularly growth and sector-specific funds, tend to perform well as companies generate higher profits. In contrast, during economic downturns, defensive funds, such as consumer staples or healthcare funds, may offer stability. Fixed-income funds, including government and corporate bond funds, perform well in low-interest-rate environments but may decline when interest rates rise. Investors should assess market trends, interest rate expectations, and economic indicators to select funds that align with prevailing market conditions. A well-balanced mutual fund portfolio considers both short-term market trends and long-term economic cycles to optimize returns.

CHAPTER 7

RETIREMENT ACCOUNTS AND TAX-ADVANTAGED INVESTMENTS

TRADITIONAL VS. ROTH IRAS

Individual Retirement Accounts (IRAs) are among the most popular tax-advantaged investment vehicles available to individuals seeking to save for retirement. IRAs allow investors to grow their money in a tax-efficient manner while benefiting from long-term compounding. The two primary types of IRAs—Traditional IRAs and Roth IRAs—differ in how they treat contributions, withdrawals, and taxation. Understanding the differences between these two accounts is essential for retirement planning, as each has unique advantages depending on an individual's income level, tax situation, and long-term financial goals.

Traditional IRAs and Roth IRAs share similarities in that they both offer tax benefits and allow for investment in a wide range of assets, including stocks, bonds, mutual funds, and ETFs. However, their primary difference lies in the timing of tax advantages. Traditional IRAs provide tax-deferred growth, meaning contributions are tax-deductible in the year they are made, but withdrawals in retirement are taxed as ordinary income. In contrast, Roth IRAs require after-tax contributions, meaning withdrawals in retirement are completely tax-free. The choice between a Traditional IRA and a Roth IRA depends on whether an individual expects their tax rate to be higher in retirement or while they are working.

Contributions and Tax Treatment

One of the key distinctions between Traditional IRAs and Roth IRAs is how contributions are handled from a tax perspective. In a Traditional IRA, contributions are tax-deductible, reducing taxable income for the year in which the contribution is made. This provides an immediate tax benefit, allowing investors to save more money upfront while deferring taxes until retirement. However, upon withdrawal, all distributions from a Traditional IRA are taxed at ordinary income tax rates.

Roth IRA contributions, on the other hand, are made with after-tax dollars, meaning they do not provide an immediate tax deduction. The advantage of a Roth IRA is that qualified withdrawals in retirement—including both the contributions and investment earnings—are completely tax-free. This feature makes Roth IRAs particularly beneficial for individuals who expect to be in a higher tax bracket in retirement, as they can take advantage of tax-free withdrawals.

Both Traditional and Roth IRAs have annual contribution limits set by the IRS. As of recent tax years, the contribution limit for both types of IRAs is $6,500 per year for individuals under age 50 and $7,500 per year for individuals age 50 and older, allowing for "catch-up" contributions. However, there are income limits that determine eligibility for Roth IRA contributions, making them unavailable to high earners.

Eligibility and Income Limits

While anyone with earned income can contribute to a Traditional IRA, the ability to deduct contributions depends on whether the individual or their spouse is covered by a workplace retirement plan. If an individual is covered by an employer-sponsored plan, such as a 401(k), the deductibility of contributions is phased out based on income level. If they are not covered by a retirement plan at work, contributions to a Traditional IRA are fully deductible regardless of income.

Roth IRAs, however, have strict income limits that determine eligibility. If an individual's income exceeds a certain threshold, they may be ineligible to contribute to a Roth IRA directly. These income limits are based on Modified Adjusted Gross Income (MAGI) and change annually based on IRS guidelines.

For single filers, Roth IRA contribution limits begin to phase out at an income level of approximately $138,000, with full ineligibility occurring at $153,000 or higher. For married couples filing jointly, the phase-out range starts at $218,000 and ends at $228,000 or higher. Individuals who exceed these income limits may still access Roth benefits using the Backdoor Roth IRA strategy, which involves contributing to a Traditional IRA and then converting it to a Roth IRA.

Withdrawal Rules and Penalties

Withdrawals from Traditional and Roth IRAs are subject to different rules, particularly regarding taxation and penalties.

Because Traditional IRAs provide tax-deferred growth, all distributions from the account in retirement are subject to ordinary income tax rates. Withdrawals taken before age 59½ may be subject to a 10% early withdrawal penalty, in addition to income taxes, unless an exception applies.

One of the biggest drawbacks of Traditional IRAs is that they have Required Minimum Distributions (RMDs). Starting at age 73, account holders must begin taking withdrawals from their Traditional IRA each year, based on life expectancy calculations provided by the IRS. These mandatory withdrawals prevent investors from deferring taxes indefinitely and ensure that the government eventually collects tax revenue from retirement accounts.

Roth IRAs, on the other hand, offer much more flexibility in withdrawals. Since contributions are made with after-tax dollars, investors can withdraw their original contributions at any time without taxes or penalties. However, to withdraw earnings tax-free, the account must be open for at least five years, and the account holder must be at least 59½ years old. Because Roth IRAs do not have RMDs, they are an excellent tool for individuals who want to pass wealth on to heirs without being forced to withdraw funds during their lifetime.

Which IRA is Best?

Deciding between a Traditional IRA and a Roth IRA depends on multiple factors, including current tax situation, expected tax rate in retirement, and financial goals.

A Traditional IRA is typically best suited for:

- Individuals who are currently in a high tax bracket and expect to be in a lower tax bracket in retirement.
- Those who need immediate tax deductions to reduce their taxable income.
- Investors who expect to withdraw money in a lower-tax environment during retirement.
- Individuals who do not mind Required Minimum Distributions (RMDs) and plan to use the funds during retirement.

A Roth IRA is generally the better choice for:

- Younger investors who are in a lower tax bracket now and expect to be in a higher tax bracket later.
- Individuals who prefer tax-free withdrawals in retirement and want to avoid RMDs.
- Those who may need to access their contributions before retirement without penalties.
- Investors who want to leave tax-free assets to heirs, as Roth IRAs do not require distributions during the account holder's lifetime.

Converting a Traditional IRA to a Roth IRA

For individuals who do not qualify for a Roth IRA due to income limits, or those who initially contributed to a Traditional IRA but later decide they want tax-free withdrawals, a Roth conversion is an option. This process involves transferring assets from a Traditional IRA to a Roth IRA and paying taxes on the converted amount in the year of conversion.

A Roth conversion can be advantageous if an individual expects their future tax rate to be higher than their current tax rate.

By paying taxes now at a lower rate, they can enjoy tax-free withdrawals later. However, the tax liability of the conversion can be significant, and investors should consider whether they have sufficient non-retirement savings to cover the taxes without dipping into their IRA funds.

401(K) AND PENSION PLANS

Employer-sponsored retirement plans, such as 401(k) plans and pension plans, play a crucial role in helping employees secure their financial future. These plans provide tax advantages, employer contributions, and long-term savings benefits that allow individuals to accumulate wealth for retirement. While both types of plans serve the same fundamental purpose of providing income after retirement, they differ significantly in how they are structured, funded, and managed.

A 401(k) plan is a defined contribution plan, meaning the employee contributes a portion of their salary into an investment account, and the final retirement benefit depends on how well those investments perform. Employers often offer matching contributions to encourage employee participation, but employees bear the investment risk and are responsible for making appropriate financial decisions.

In contrast, a pension plan is a defined benefit plan, where the employer is solely responsible for funding the plan and guaranteeing a set monthly payout in retirement. Pension benefits are typically based on a formula that considers the employee's salary history, years of service, and retirement age. Unlike a 401(k), employees have little to no control over how pension funds are invested, but they are assured a steady income for life.

Over the past few decades, pension plans have become increasingly rare in the private sector, as many employers have transitioned to 401(k) plans due to the lower financial burden and reduced long-term liabilities. However, government jobs, unionized positions, and certain large corporations still offer pension plans. Choosing between a 401(k) and a pension plan, when given the option, requires understanding the unique benefits and risks associated with each.

A 401(k) plan allows employees to contribute a percentage of their salary into a tax-advantaged account, where it grows over time. Contributions can be made in pre-tax dollars (Traditional 401(k)) or after-tax dollars (Roth 401(k)), depending on the plan's structure. The IRS sets annual contribution limits, and employers may offer matching contributions, which significantly enhance an employee's retirement savings.

One of the major advantages of a 401(k) is the flexibility it provides. Employees can choose their contribution level, adjust their investment portfolio, and withdraw funds under specific conditions. However, the downside is that the final retirement balance depends on market performance, making it less predictable than a pension plan. Employees also need to actively manage their investments to ensure they are on track for a secure retirement.

A pension plan, on the other hand, provides retirees with a fixed income stream for life, removing the uncertainty associated with stock market fluctuations. Employers fund and manage these plans, ensuring that employees receive guaranteed payments upon retirement. The amount an employee receives is determined by a set formula that considers factors such as years of service and final salary.

The most significant advantage of a pension plan is the security and predictability it offers. Unlike a 401(k), where retirees must carefully budget their savings, pension recipients receive a steady, predetermined amount each month, making financial planning easier. However, the main drawback is that employees have no control over their pension investments, and pension benefits may not be as flexible as a 401(k) in terms of accessing funds.

Another important factor to consider is vesting schedules. In a 401(k) plan, employee contributions are always fully vested, meaning they belong to the employee from the moment they are deposited. However, employer contributions may be subject to a vesting schedule, requiring employees to work for a certain number of years before gaining full ownership of those funds. Pension plans also have vesting requirements, and employees typically need to work for the company for a minimum number of years (often five to ten) to qualify for full pension benefits.

When it comes to tax treatment, both 401(k) and pension plans offer tax-deferred growth, but withdrawals are taxed differently. Traditional 401(k) withdrawals are taxed as ordinary income, while Roth 401(k) withdrawals are tax-free in retirement if certain conditions are met. Pension payments are taxed as income when received, as contributions are made with pre-tax dollars.

Another key consideration is Required Minimum Distributions (RMDs). Both Traditional 401(k) plans and pension plans require retirees to start taking distributions at age 73, ensuring that funds are gradually withdrawn and taxed. Roth 401(k)s also have RMD requirements, but funds can be rolled into a Roth IRA, which does not require minimum distributions.

In terms of accessibility, 401(k) plans allow for loans and hardship withdrawals, though there are restrictions and potential penalties for early withdrawals before age 59½. Pension plans do not allow employees to borrow from their future benefits, making them less flexible in case of financial emergencies.

For individuals who have the option of both a 401(k) and a pension plan, the best approach is to maximize contributions to both if financially feasible. Having both types of retirement income creates a balanced strategy, combining the security of a pension with the growth potential of a 401(k).

Overall, 401(k) plans and pension plans each offer distinct benefits and challenges. A 401(k) provides flexibility, personal control, and investment growth potential, but it also requires careful financial management. A pension plan offers guaranteed income and stability but lacks investment control and may have strict vesting requirements. The best choice depends on an individual's career stability, financial goals, and risk tolerance. Understanding these retirement options helps employees make informed decisions about securing their financial future.

TAX TREATMENT OF INVESTMENTS

Investments are subject to various tax rules that can significantly impact overall returns. Understanding how different types of investments are taxed is essential for making informed financial decisions and optimizing after-tax income. Tax treatment varies depending on the type of investment, the duration of holding, and the account in which the investment is held. Some investments receive preferential tax treatment, while others are taxed at ordinary income rates.

Capital Gains and Losses

When an investor sells an asset for more than its purchase price, the profit is known as a capital gain. Conversely, if the asset is sold for less than its purchase price, it results in a capital loss. The tax rate applied to capital gains depends on the holding period of the investment. If an asset is held for one year or less, the gain is classified as a short-term capital gain and is taxed at the investor's ordinary income tax rate, which can be as high as 37% for high-income earners. If an asset is held for more than one year, it qualifies for long-term capital gains treatment, which benefits from lower tax rates of 0%, 15%, or 20%, depending on the investor's income level.

Capital losses can be used to offset capital gains, reducing taxable income. If an investor has more losses than gains, they can deduct up to $3,000 per year against ordinary income, with any remaining losses carried forward to future tax years. This strategy, known as tax-loss harvesting, helps investors minimize tax liability by strategically selling underperforming assets.

Dividend Taxation

Dividends are payments made by corporations to shareholders as a distribution of profits. The tax treatment of dividends depends on whether they are classified as qualified or non-qualified (ordinary) dividends.

Qualified dividends are taxed at the lower long-term capital gains rates of 0%, 15%, or 20%, provided that the investor has held the stock for a minimum required period. These dividends typically come from U.S. corporations and certain foreign companies that meet IRS criteria.

Non-qualified (ordinary) dividends are taxed at the investor's ordinary income tax rate, which is often higher than the capital gains rate. These dividends include those paid by real estate investment trusts (REITs), master limited partnerships (MLPs), and certain foreign corporations that do not meet IRS qualifications for preferential tax treatment.

Investors seeking tax-efficient income often prefer stocks that pay qualified dividends, as they provide a lower tax burden compared to ordinary dividends or bond interest.

Tax Treatment of Bonds and Fixed-Income Investments

Bonds generate interest income, which is generally taxed as ordinary income, making them less tax-efficient compared to stocks. The tax treatment of bond income depends on the type of bond issued.

Corporate bonds pay interest that is fully taxable at both the federal and state levels. Investors holding corporate bonds in taxable accounts must pay ordinary income tax rates on the interest they receive.

Municipal bonds, issued by state and local governments, provide tax-free interest income at the federal level. If the investor resides in the same state where the bond was issued, the interest may also be exempt from state and local taxes. This tax-exempt status makes municipal bonds attractive to high-income investors seeking to minimize their tax liability.

U.S. Treasury bonds, notes, and bills pay interest that is taxable at the federal level but exempt from state and local taxes. This feature makes them appealing to investors living in high-tax states.

Some bonds, known as taxable municipal bonds or high-yield corporate bonds, do not qualify for tax-exempt status and are taxed like ordinary income. Investors must consider the after-tax return when comparing bond investments, as tax-exempt municipal bonds can provide higher net returns for certain investors despite offering lower nominal interest rates.

Tax Treatment of Retirement Accounts

Retirement accounts offer tax advantages that help investors grow their wealth more efficiently. The two main types of retirement accounts—tax-deferred accounts and tax-free accounts—have different rules for taxation of contributions, withdrawals, and investment gains.

Traditional IRAs and 401(k) plans provide tax-deferred growth, meaning contributions are made with pre-tax dollars, reducing taxable income in the year of contribution. Investments within these accounts grow without immediate taxation, but withdrawals in retirement are taxed as ordinary income. Required Minimum Distributions (RMDs) must begin at age 73, forcing retirees to withdraw and pay taxes on a portion of their account balance each year.

Roth IRAs and Roth 401(k) plans offer tax-free growth, as contributions are made with after-tax dollars. While there is no upfront tax deduction, all qualified withdrawals—including earnings—are completely tax-free in retirement. Roth accounts also do not have RMD requirements, making them ideal for long-term tax-free wealth accumulation.

The choice between tax-deferred and tax-free retirement accounts depends on expected future tax rates. Individuals who anticipate higher taxes in retirement may benefit from a Roth IRA, while those in higher tax brackets during their working years may prefer a Traditional IRA or 401(k) to reduce their taxable income.

Tax Treatment of Real Estate Investments

Real estate investments provide unique tax benefits, including depreciation deductions, capital gains advantages, and tax-deferred exchanges. Rental income is taxed as ordinary income, but investors can deduct mortgage interest, property taxes, maintenance costs, and depreciation, reducing taxable income.

One of the most valuable tax benefits in real estate is depreciation, which allows investors to deduct a portion of the property's value each year, even if the property appreciates in market value. Depreciation can significantly reduce taxable income, though it is subject to recapture tax upon sale.

Real estate investors who sell properties may be subject to capital gains tax, but they can defer taxes using a 1031 exchange, which allows reinvestment of proceeds into another investment property without immediate tax consequences. This strategy helps investors defer capital gains indefinitely while continuing to grow their portfolio.

Taxation of Investment Funds

Mutual funds and exchange-traded funds (ETFs) have distinct tax implications based on their structure and trading mechanisms.

Mutual funds generate capital gains distributions, which are taxable to investors even if they did not sell shares. This occurs when fund managers sell holdings within the fund, creating taxable events for shareholders. Actively managed mutual funds tend to have higher turnover and larger taxable distributions, making them less tax-efficient.

ETFs, on the other hand, are generally more tax-efficient because they use an in-kind creation and redemption process, reducing the likelihood of taxable distributions. Index-based ETFs have minimal trading activity, resulting in lower capital gains distributions compared to actively managed mutual funds.

Tax Considerations for Alternative Investments

Alternative investments, such as hedge funds, commodities, and private equity, often have complex tax structures that require specialized knowledge.

Hedge funds generate a mix of short-term and long-term capital gains, dividend income, and interest income, leading to varied tax treatment. Investors in hedge funds may also receive K-1 tax forms, requiring additional tax reporting.

Commodities and futures contracts are taxed differently from traditional investments. Gains from futures contracts are subject to the 60/40 rule, meaning 60% of gains are taxed at long-term capital gains rates and 40% are taxed at short-term rates, regardless of holding period.

Private equity and venture capital investments often have long holding periods and may be subject to carried interest taxation, which allows fund managers to pay capital gains tax rates on earnings instead of higher ordinary income rates.

CHAPTER 8
MARGIN AND TRADING ACCOUNTS

CASH VS. MARGIN ACCOUNTS

When investors open a brokerage account, they typically choose between a cash account and a margin account. These two types of accounts differ in how trades are funded, the risks involved, and the opportunities they provide. A cash account requires investors to fully pay for their securities purchases, meaning they cannot borrow money to buy stocks or other assets. In contrast, a margin account allows investors to borrow money from the brokerage firm to buy securities, leveraging their investments to potentially enhance returns but also increasing risk.

Understanding the differences between cash and margin accounts is essential for traders and investors to determine which type of account best suits their financial goals and risk tolerance. Each account type has its own benefits, drawbacks, and regulatory requirements that affect how trades are executed and managed.

Cash Accounts

A cash account is the most basic type of brokerage account in which all transactions must be fully funded by the investor's own money. When an investor purchases a stock, bond, or other security in a cash account, they must pay the full amount of the purchase price before the trade settles. Unlike a margin account, there is no borrowing involved, which eliminates the risks associated with leverage.

One of the main advantages of a cash account is that it prevents investors from accumulating debt. Since all trades are funded with available cash, investors cannot lose more money than they have deposited into their account. This makes cash accounts ideal for conservative investors who prefer to limit risk and avoid the potential for margin calls.

Cash accounts are subject to the settlement period rule, which means that when an investor sells a security, the proceeds from the sale are not immediately available for reinvestment. Instead, the funds must go through a T+2 settlement cycle, meaning the transaction is completed two business days after the trade date. This delay in access to funds can impact active traders who wish to make frequent transactions.

Another limitation of cash accounts is the good faith violation rule, which applies when an investor purchases a security with funds that have not yet fully settled from a previous sale. If an investor sells a stock and immediately uses the proceeds to buy another stock before the original sale has settled, it results in a violation. If repeated violations occur, the brokerage may restrict the investor's trading activity.

Cash accounts are well-suited for long-term investors, beginners, and those who prefer a lower-risk approach to trading. Since there is no borrowing involved, investors do not pay interest on their trades and are not subject to margin maintenance requirements.

Margin Accounts

A margin account allows investors to borrow money from the brokerage to buy securities, increasing their purchasing power. This borrowing is known as margin trading, and it allows investors to leverage their capital to potentially amplify returns. However, margin trading also increases risk, as losses can exceed the initial investment.

When an investor opens a margin account, the brokerage firm extends credit based on the value of the assets in the account. The investor must deposit an initial amount, known as the initial margin requirement, which is typically at least 50% of the purchase price of the securities according to Federal Reserve Regulation T. This means that if an investor wants to buy $10,000 worth of stock, they must deposit at least $5,000, with the brokerage lending the remaining amount.

Once securities are purchased on margin, the investor must maintain a minimum account balance, known as the maintenance margin, which is typically 25% of the total market value of the securities. If the account balance falls below this level due to a decline in the value of the securities, the broker will issue a margin call, requiring the investor to deposit additional funds or sell assets to bring the account back up to the required level.

One of the major advantages of a margin account is the potential for higher returns. Since investors can buy more shares than they could with just their own cash, gains are magnified when stock prices increase. Additionally, margin accounts offer greater flexibility, allowing for short selling and options trading, which are not available in cash accounts.

However, the risks associated with margin trading are significant. Losses are also magnified, meaning that if the value of the securities declines, the investor can lose more than their original investment. If an investor fails to meet a margin call, the brokerage has the right to sell securities from the account without prior notice, potentially at a loss.

Margin accounts also involve interest costs, as the brokerage charges interest on the borrowed funds. Interest rates on margin loans vary by brokerage and are influenced by factors such as market conditions and the amount borrowed. These costs can reduce overall profitability, especially in volatile markets.

Key Differences

One of the primary differences between cash and margin accounts is the use of leverage. In a cash account, all purchases must be fully paid for using the investor's own money, while a margin account allows for borrowing, enabling investors to take larger positions than their available cash would allow.

Margin accounts also offer greater trading flexibility, as they allow for short selling, options trading, and day trading strategies that are not available in cash accounts. Short selling involves borrowing shares and selling them in anticipation of a price decline, aiming to buy them back later at a lower price. This strategy carries high risk, as losses can be unlimited if the stock price rises instead of falls.

In terms of risk, cash accounts are generally safer because they do not expose investors to the risk of margin calls or forced liquidations. Investors in cash accounts can only lose the money they deposit, whereas margin traders can lose more than their initial investment if their leveraged positions decline in value.

Another key difference is in the settlement period for trades. In a cash account, an investor must wait for the funds from a sale to settle before reinvesting. In contrast, a margin account allows for immediate reinvestment of sale proceeds, providing greater liquidity and efficiency for active traders.

Regulatory requirements also differ between the two account types. Margin accounts are subject to stricter regulations, including minimum margin requirements set by the Financial Industry Regulatory Authority (FINRA) and the Federal Reserve. These regulations are designed to protect both investors and brokers from excessive risk-taking.

Who Should Use a Cash Account?

Cash accounts are best suited for long-term investors, conservative traders, and beginners who want to minimize risk and avoid debt. Since cash accounts do not allow for borrowing, they prevent investors from overextending themselves and accumulating losses beyond their initial investment. Investors who follow a buy-and-hold strategy or who are saving for retirement often find cash accounts to be the best choice, as they provide a simple, straightforward approach to investing.

Cash accounts are also ideal for investors who do not engage in frequent trading or short-term speculation. Since there is no risk of a margin call or interest payments on borrowed funds, investors can focus on steady, long-term growth without the pressure of market fluctuations.

Who Should Use a Margin Account?

Margin accounts are more suitable for experienced traders, active investors, and those who understand the risks of leverage. Traders who engage in short selling, options trading, or day trading often use margin accounts to take advantage of increased buying power and flexibility. Investors who seek higher potential returns and are comfortable managing market risk may also benefit from margin accounts, as they provide opportunities to amplify gains.

However, margin trading requires discipline, risk management, and a clear understanding of market conditions. Investors must be prepared for the possibility of margin calls, interest costs, and rapid losses if market conditions turn against them. Proper risk controls, such as setting stop-loss orders and diversifying investments, are essential for managing the risks associated with margin trading.

MARGIN REQUIREMENTS AND MAINTENANCE

Margin requirements refer to the minimum amount of money an investor must deposit into their brokerage account when trading on margin. These requirements are set by regulatory bodies such as the Federal Reserve Board (Regulation T), the Financial Industry Regulatory Authority (FINRA), and individual brokerage firms. Margin requirements ensure that investors maintain a sufficient amount of equity in their accounts to cover potential losses and prevent excessive borrowing.

There are three main types of margin requirements: initial margin requirement, maintenance margin requirement, and house margin requirement. Each of these requirements serves a different purpose in ensuring that investors manage their risk appropriately when trading on margin.

The initial margin requirement is the amount an investor must deposit before executing a margin trade. According to Regulation T, investors must deposit at least 50% of the total purchase price when buying securities on margin. This means that if an investor wants to purchase $10,000 worth of stock, they must deposit at least $5,000 of their own funds, while the brokerage lends the remaining $5,000. Some brokerage firms may require a higher initial margin, depending on the investor's experience level and the volatility of the securities being purchased.

The maintenance margin requirement is the minimum amount of equity an investor must maintain in their margin account after the trade has been executed. The FINRA minimum maintenance margin requirement is 25% of the total market value of the securities held in the account. However, brokerage firms often set their own, higher maintenance margin requirements, typically around 30-40%.

If the value of an investor's margin account falls below the maintenance margin requirement, the brokerage firm will issue a margin call, requiring the investor to deposit additional funds or sell securities to restore the account balance. Failing to meet a margin call can result in the forced liquidation of securities by the brokerage, potentially at a loss.

The house margin requirement refers to additional margin requirements set by brokerage firms, which may be stricter than the regulatory minimums. Some firms impose higher margin requirements for volatile stocks, leveraged ETFs, and options trading, reducing their risk exposure. House margin requirements vary by brokerage and can change depending on market conditions.

How Margin Maintenance Works

Once an investor has met the initial margin requirement and completed a margin trade, they must continuously monitor their account to ensure it remains above the maintenance margin level. The maintenance margin ensures that investors have enough equity in their accounts to cover potential losses, reducing the risk of default.

Margin maintenance is calculated using the following formula:

The maintenance margin is expressed as a percentage of the total market value of the securities in the account. If the equity in the account falls below this level due to a decline in stock prices, the investor will receive a margin call.

For example, suppose an investor purchases $20,000 worth of stock using $10,000 of their own money and $10,000 borrowed on margin. If the maintenance margin requirement is 25%, the investor must maintain at least $5,000 in equity (25% of

$20,000). If the stock's market value drops to $15,000, the investor's equity becomes $5,000 ($15,000 - $10,000 loan), which is still above the maintenance margin requirement. However, if the stock's value declines further to $12,000, the equity falls to $2,000 ($12,000 - $10,000 loan), which is below the required $3,000 (25% of $12,000). At this point, the brokerage will issue a margin call demanding that the investor deposit additional funds or sell securities to restore the required equity level.

Margin Calls and Liquidation

A margin call occurs when an investor's account equity falls below the maintenance margin requirement, requiring them to take immediate action. When a margin call is issued, the investor has two options:

- Deposit additional funds or securities to bring the account back up to the required margin level.
- Sell securities to reduce the amount of the margin loan and restore the required equity percentage.

If the investor fails to meet the margin call, the brokerage firm has the right to liquidate securities in the account to cover the shortfall. The brokerage can do this without prior notice, potentially selling securities at an unfavorable price. Forced liquidations can result in significant losses, especially in a declining market.

Investors can avoid margin calls by monitoring their account balance regularly, maintaining a buffer above the minimum maintenance margin, and using stop-loss orders to limit potential losses.

Risks Associated with Margin Trading

While margin trading offers the potential for higher returns, it also comes with significant risks. One of the most notable risks is amplified losses. Since investors are borrowing money to trade, losses are magnified if the market moves against them. A small decline in stock prices can lead to large losses, particularly if the investor is forced to liquidate positions to meet a margin call.

Another major risk is forced liquidation. If an investor fails to meet a margin call, the brokerage firm can sell securities without consulting the investor, potentially at a loss. Since brokers prioritize protecting their capital, they will often liquidate assets as soon as an account falls below maintenance margin levels, sometimes selling investments that the investor intended to hold long term.

Margin traders also face interest costs, as they must pay interest on the borrowed funds. The interest rate on margin loans varies by brokerage and is influenced by factors such as market conditions, loan amount, and account type. Interest charges can eat into profits and create additional financial pressure, particularly in volatile markets.

Additionally, margin trading introduces psychological risks, as the possibility of large gains or losses can lead to emotional decision-making. Investors who trade on margin must have a high level of discipline, risk tolerance, and financial awareness to manage their positions effectively.

Regulatory Protections and Margin Rules

To prevent excessive risk-taking and protect both investors and brokerage firms, margin trading is subject to strict regulatory oversight. Several key regulations govern margin trading:

- Regulation T (Reg T): Enforced by the Federal Reserve Board, this regulation sets the initial margin requirement at 50%, limiting the amount investors can borrow when making a margin trade.
- FINRA Rule 4210: Establishes the minimum maintenance margin requirement of 25%, ensuring that investors maintain a certain level of equity in their accounts.
- House Margin Requirements: Individual brokerage firms often impose stricter margin requirements, particularly for volatile securities, leveraged ETFs, and options trading.

Brokerages may also increase margin requirements during periods of high market volatility, requiring investors to maintain higher equity levels in their accounts. These adjustments help prevent widespread forced liquidations that could further destabilize the market.

RISKS OF LEVERAGED TRADING

Leveraged trading involves borrowing money or using financial instruments such as margin accounts, options, or leveraged ETFs to increase potential returns. While leverage can amplify gains, it also significantly increases risk. The use of borrowed capital means that even small price movements can result in substantial losses, potentially exceeding the investor's original investment. Understanding the risks associated with leveraged trading is essential for investors who seek to use this strategy while managing their exposure to financial loss.

Amplified Losses

One of the primary risks of leveraged trading is that losses are magnified in the same way as gains. When an investor uses leverage to increase their position size, even minor price fluctuations can result in significant financial consequences.

For example, if an investor buys $10,000 worth of stock using $5,000 of their own money and $5,000 borrowed on margin, a 10% drop in stock price ($1,000 loss) would result in a 20% decline in equity, since the investor still owes the brokerage the full $5,000 loan. If the stock price continues to decline, the investor could face a margin call or a total loss of their investment.

Unlike cash trading, where the maximum loss is limited to the amount invested, leveraged trading can wipe out an investor's entire portfolio quickly. In extreme cases, investors may even owe money to their brokerage if losses exceed their account balance.

Margin Calls and Forced Liquidation

When investors trade using margin, they must maintain a minimum level of equity in their accounts to comply with brokerage and regulatory requirements. If the value of their positions falls below this required level, they receive a margin call, which requires them to deposit additional funds or liquidate assets.

If an investor fails to meet a margin call, the brokerage has the right to sell securities without the investor's consent, often at unfavorable prices. This forced liquidation can lead to larger losses than expected because securities may be sold during a market downturn, locking in losses that might have been avoided with a recovery.

Margin calls are particularly dangerous during market volatility, as price swings can quickly push an investor's equity below the maintenance margin, triggering a series of forced sell-offs. This can create a chain reaction where falling prices force liquidations, further driving prices down and exacerbating market instability.

Interest Costs on Borrowed Funds

Using leverage involves borrowing money, which means investors must pay interest on their margin loans. The interest rates on margin loans vary by brokerage and depend on factors such as account balance, prevailing market conditions, and the amount borrowed.

Unlike a traditional loan, where repayments are structured, margin loan interest accrues daily and is added to the investor's account balance. If an investor holds a margin position for an extended period, the cost of interest can significantly erode potential gains and turn a profitable trade into a loss.

For example, if an investor borrows $50,000 at a 10% annual interest rate, they will owe $5,000 in interest per year just to maintain their position. If the market does not perform as expected, the investor may struggle to generate sufficient returns to cover both interest costs and capital appreciation.

Volatility and Market Risk

Leveraged trading amplifies exposure to market volatility, making it riskier than traditional investing. In highly volatile markets, price swings can trigger stop-loss orders, margin calls, or forced liquidations, leading to substantial financial losses.

Leveraged ETFs, for example, use derivatives to magnify daily price movements, but their structure makes them unsuitable for long-term holding. Over time, the compounding effect of daily price fluctuations can cause leveraged ETFs to diverge significantly from their intended performance, leading to unexpected losses for investors who do not actively manage their positions.

During periods of extreme market fluctuations, such as economic downturns or geopolitical crises, leveraged traders face heightened risk. Markets can move against leveraged positions rapidly and unpredictably, making it difficult to exit trades at desired prices.

Psychological and Emotional Risks

Leveraged trading can create emotional stress and impulsive decision-making, leading to poor trading discipline and panic selling. Since leverage increases both potential gains and losses, traders often experience heightened emotions when markets move sharply.

For many investors, seeing their portfolio swing in value dramatically can lead to irrational decision-making, such as holding onto losing positions for too long or panic-selling during a market downturn. The temptation to chase losses by adding more leverage can result in even greater financial damage.

Successful leveraged trading requires a high degree of emotional control, discipline, and risk management, as the temptation to overtrade or double down on losses can lead to catastrophic financial consequences.

Overleveraging and Portfolio Instability

Overleveraging occurs when traders take on too much debt relative to their account balance, increasing the risk of total financial ruin. When an investor borrows excessively, they become highly vulnerable to even small market fluctuations.

A single unexpected market downturn can wipe out an overleveraged trader's entire portfolio, leaving them with outstanding debt. This is particularly common in highly speculative trades, such as futures contracts and forex trading, where leverage ratios can be as high as 100:1 or more.

Diversification is critical for reducing risk, but leveraged traders often concentrate their capital in a few high-risk positions, making their portfolio highly unstable. If one trade moves against them, their entire investment strategy can collapse.

Liquidity Risk and Trade Execution

Liquidity risk refers to the inability to exit a leveraged position at a desired price due to a lack of market participants willing to buy or sell. This can be particularly problematic during market crashes or sudden price swings, when prices move too quickly for traders to react.

Some financial instruments, such as options and futures contracts, have lower liquidity than stocks, meaning that executing trades at favorable prices can be difficult. If a leveraged trader is unable to close a position in time, they may suffer larger-than-expected losses due to price slippage.

Additionally, during periods of high volatility, brokerage firms may suspend margin trading or adjust margin requirements, limiting the ability of traders to manage their positions effectively. These sudden rule changes can disrupt trading strategies and force traders into unplanned liquidations.

Regulatory and Broker Risk

Leverage is highly regulated, and brokers set specific margin requirements, risk controls, and trading restrictions to protect both themselves and their clients. In extreme market conditions, brokers can increase margin requirements or restrict certain trades, catching traders off guard.

For example, during the GameStop (GME) short squeeze in early 2021, several brokers restricted margin trading and imposed limits on certain stocks, preventing traders from managing their positions. This resulted in forced liquidations and losses for many leveraged traders who were unable to adjust their portfolios.

Additionally, if a brokerage firm experiences financial trouble or becomes insolvent, traders may face difficulties accessing their accounts, leading to potential losses. Although regulations exist to protect investor funds, there is always a risk of broker mismanagement or operational failure.

CHAPTER 9
REGULATIONS AND COMPLIANCE

SEC AND FINRA RULES

The Securities and Exchange Commission (SEC) and the Financial Industry Regulatory Authority (FINRA) are the primary regulatory bodies responsible for overseeing the securities markets in the United States. Their roles are essential in maintaining market integrity, investor protection, and compliance with federal securities laws. While the SEC is a government agency with broad regulatory authority, FINRA operates as a self-regulatory organization (SRO) that enforces rules governing broker-dealers and financial professionals.

SEC regulations focus on financial disclosures, fraud prevention, and compliance with securities laws, while FINRA supervises brokerage firms, establishes rules for fair trading, and ensures that financial professionals adhere to ethical standards. Both organizations play a crucial role in protecting investors from market manipulation, ensuring transparency, and maintaining orderly financial markets.

Securities and Exchange Commission (SEC) Rules

The SEC enforces laws and regulations that apply to publicly traded companies, brokerage firms, investment advisors, and financial institutions. It has the authority to investigate securities fraud, impose penalties for violations, and regulate financial reporting to ensure market participants comply with established standards.

1. Financial Disclosure and Reporting Requirements

Public companies must file regular financial reports with the SEC to provide transparency to investors and the general public. These filings include annual and quarterly reports, earnings disclosures, and event-driven reports, which help investors evaluate a company's financial health and decision-making. The Form 10-K is an annual report that contains audited financial statements, management's discussion of financial conditions, and potential risk factors affecting the company's operations. The Form 10-Q is filed quarterly and includes unaudited financial updates, recent developments, and revenue changes over three-month periods. If a company experiences a significant corporate event such as a merger, acquisition, executive resignation, or lawsuit, it must submit Form 8-K immediately.

Failure to file accurate and timely reports can result in SEC enforcement actions, fines, and even delisting from stock exchanges. If a company is found to have manipulated earnings reports, hidden financial losses, or misrepresented its financial position, it can face legal consequences, including civil lawsuits and criminal charges. The SEC frequently conducts audits and investigations to ensure companies comply with financial reporting standards and do not engage in misleading accounting practices.

2. Insider Trading Regulations

Insider trading occurs when individuals buy or sell securities based on non-public material information, giving them an unfair advantage over ordinary investors. The SEC enforces strict insider trading laws to prevent executives, employees, and other individuals with privileged access to financial data from exploiting confidential corporate information for personal gain. High-profile insider trading cases have resulted in multi-million dollar fines, imprisonment, and trading bans for violators.

To monitor insider trading, public companies must file Form 4 with the SEC whenever company insiders, such as executives or board members, buy or sell shares of their own company. These disclosures allow investors to track transactions made by company leadership, helping identify potential conflicts of interest or suspicious trading activity. Insider trading violations not only result in financial penalties and criminal charges but also damage investor confidence in the fairness of financial markets.

3. Market Manipulation and Fraud Prevention

The SEC actively investigates and enforces regulations against market manipulation, securities fraud, and deceptive trading practices. Market manipulation occurs when traders or firms artificially influence stock prices through pump-and-dump schemes, wash trading, or spoofing. In a pump-and-dump scheme, promoters hype up a stock with misleading information to drive up its price, only to sell their holdings at a profit before the price collapses.

Wash trading involves executing trades between accounts controlled by the same entity to create an illusion of higher trading volume and attract unsuspecting investors. Spoofing occurs when traders place large orders with no intention of executing them, misleading other market participants about supply and demand. The SEC works with federal agencies and exchanges to detect and penalize firms or individuals engaged in these fraudulent activities.

Fraudulent financial reporting is another focus of SEC enforcement, with companies facing severe penalties for falsifying revenue, hiding expenses, or inflating profits to mislead investors. The SEC uses forensic accounting techniques to identify irregularities in financial statements and holds executives accountable for corporate misconduct.

4. Regulation Best Interest (Reg BI) and Fiduciary Duty
The SEC requires financial professionals to prioritize their clients' best interests when recommending investment products, under the Regulation Best Interest (Reg BI) rule. Broker-dealers must disclose conflicts of interest, fees, and risks associated with financial products, ensuring that investors receive fair and transparent advice.

Investment advisors registered with the SEC must adhere to a fiduciary duty, which means they are legally obligated to act in their clients' best interests at all times. Fiduciary duty includes providing full disclosure of investment risks, avoiding conflicts of interest, and executing trades that align with an investor's financial goals and risk tolerance.

Financial Industry Regulatory Authority (FINRA) Rules

FINRA is a self-regulatory organization that oversees brokerage firms, registered representatives, and trading practices. It enforces ethical standards, licenses financial professionals, and ensures compliance with securities laws through audits, investigations, and arbitration proceedings.

1. Licensing and Registration Requirements

FINRA requires individuals who work in the securities industry to pass licensing exams and register with the organization before conducting investment activities. The most common exam is the Series 7 (General Securities Representative Exam), which qualifies individuals to sell stocks, bonds, and other securities. Financial professionals may also need to pass the Series 63 (Uniform Securities Agent State Law Exam) or Series 65 (Investment Adviser Law Exam) to comply with state regulations.

Brokerage firms must register with FINRA and comply with financial reporting, record-keeping, and ethical conduct requirements. FINRA conducts background checks on registered representatives to ensure they meet industry standards and have no history of fraud, misconduct, or financial mismanagement.

2. Margin and Short Selling Regulations

FINRA enforces margin trading rules to prevent excessive leverage and financial instability. Under FINRA Rule 4210, investors must maintain a minimum equity level in their margin accounts to avoid excessive borrowing and reduce default risk. Short selling, which involves selling borrowed shares in anticipation of a price decline, is also regulated to prevent market manipulation and naked short selling.

Brokers must adhere to strict reporting requirements when executing short sales, ensuring that traders locate and borrow shares before shorting them. Failure to comply with these rules can lead to penalties, trading restrictions, and increased margin requirements.

3. Suitability and Investor Protection Rules

FINRA enforces suitability requirements under FINRA Rule 2111, ensuring that brokers recommend investments that align with a client's financial situation, investment objectives, and risk tolerance. Brokers must conduct due diligence before recommending securities, disclose risks, and ensure that investment products suit the client's needs.

If brokers engage in excessive trading (churning), misleading sales practices, or unauthorized transactions, FINRA can impose disciplinary actions, fines, or license suspensions. Investors who suffer losses due to broker misconduct can file complaints through FINRA's arbitration and dispute resolution process.

ANTI-MONEY LAUNDERING (AML) AND KNOW YOUR CUSTOMER (KYC)

The financial industry is a major target for money laundering and other financial crimes, making Anti-Money Laundering (AML) and Know Your Customer (KYC) regulations essential for preventing illegal activities. These regulations help financial institutions detect and prevent money laundering, terrorist financing, fraud, and other illicit activities by requiring institutions to verify customer identities, monitor transactions, and report suspicious activities.

AML and KYC regulations are enforced by financial regulators worldwide, including the Financial Crimes Enforcement

Network (FinCEN) in the United States, the Financial Action Task Force (FATF) internationally, the Securities and Exchange Commission (SEC), and the Financial Industry Regulatory Authority (FINRA). Non-compliance with AML and KYC laws can result in severe penalties, including fines, license suspensions, and even criminal charges.

Anti-Money Laundering (AML) Regulations

AML regulations are designed to identify, prevent, and report suspicious financial activities that could be linked to money laundering or terrorist financing. Money laundering is the process of disguising illegally obtained money by making it appear as though it originates from a legitimate source. Criminal organizations, corrupt officials, and terrorists use money laundering schemes to hide illicit funds and integrate them into the financial system.

AML laws require financial institutions, including banks, brokerage firms, and investment firms, to implement robust compliance programs to detect and prevent money laundering. These programs involve transaction monitoring, customer verification, record-keeping, and reporting obligations to law enforcement authorities.

One of the primary AML laws in the United States is the Bank Secrecy Act (BSA), which requires financial institutions to maintain records of transactions and file reports for suspicious or large financial activities. Under the BSA, financial institutions must comply with the following key requirements:

1. Suspicious Activity Reporting (SARs)

Financial institutions are required to file a Suspicious Activity Report (SAR) with FinCEN whenever they detect potentially fraudulent or suspicious transactions. These reports help law enforcement track and investigate criminal activities related to money laundering, terrorism financing, fraud, or other illicit financial activities.

Suspicious activity can include large cash deposits, frequent wire transfers to high-risk jurisdictions, attempts to avoid reporting thresholds, or transactions that lack a clear economic purpose. Financial firms must have internal systems in place to monitor account activity and flag transactions that deviate from a customer's usual financial behavior.

Failure to report suspicious transactions can result in significant penalties, regulatory fines, and reputational damage for financial institutions. Regulators closely monitor compliance, and firms that fail to file SARs may face regulatory scrutiny.

2. Currency Transaction Reporting (CTR)

Under the Bank Secrecy Act (BSA), financial institutions must file a Currency Transaction Report (CTR) for cash transactions exceeding $10,000 in a single day. The goal of this requirement is to prevent criminals from using financial institutions to launder large sums of money without detection.

Structuring, or breaking down large transactions into smaller amounts to avoid reporting requirements, is illegal. Financial institutions must have systems in place to detect patterns of structuring and other methods used to evade CTR requirements.

3. Customer Due Diligence (CDD) and Enhanced Due Diligence (EDD)

Customer Due Diligence (CDD) is a critical component of AML compliance, requiring financial institutions to identify and verify customers before establishing a business relationship. CDD ensures that financial firms know who their customers are, what types of transactions they engage in, and whether their activities pose a risk of money laundering or terrorism financing.

In cases where customers present higher risks—such as politically exposed persons (PEPs), high-net-worth individuals, or entities operating in high-risk countries—financial institutions must conduct Enhanced Due Diligence (EDD). EDD involves additional verification procedures, deeper transaction monitoring, and continuous risk assessment to prevent financial crime.

CDD and EDD help financial institutions detect shell companies, illicit financial networks, and suspicious business activities that could be linked to money laundering or organized crime.

Know Your Customer (KYC) Regulations

KYC regulations require financial institutions to verify the identities of their clients and assess their risk profiles before allowing them to engage in financial transactions. KYC is a fundamental part of AML compliance and is designed to prevent criminals from using fake identities or fraudulent accounts to conduct illicit activities.

The KYC process typically involves three main components: Customer Identification Program (CIP), Customer Due Diligence (CDD), and ongoing monitoring.

1. Customer Identification Program (CIP)

The Customer Identification Program (CIP) is the first step in KYC compliance, requiring financial institutions to collect and verify personal information from new customers before opening accounts.

CIP verification includes collecting:

- Full legal name
- Date of birth
- Address (residential or business)
- Government-issued identification (passport, driver's license, national ID)
- Taxpayer identification number (Social Security Number, Employer Identification Number)

Financial firms must ensure that customer-provided information is accurate and authentic. Many firms use electronic identity verification (eIDV) systems, biometrics, and third-party databases to cross-check customer identities and detect fraudulent applications.

2. Customer Risk Profiling and Risk-Based Approach

Once a customer's identity is verified, financial institutions assess their risk level based on their financial behavior, occupation, geographic location, and transaction history. Customers are categorized into low-risk, medium-risk, or high-risk profiles, with enhanced monitoring applied to high-risk accounts.

A risk-based approach ensures that firms allocate more resources to high-risk customers and transactions while applying standard monitoring to lower-risk individuals. This helps prevent financial crimes while minimizing unnecessary compliance burdens.

3. Ongoing Monitoring and Transaction Surveillance

KYC compliance does not end once an account is opened. Financial institutions must conduct continuous monitoring of customer transactions to detect unusual patterns, large transfers, or changes in account behavior. Advanced analytics and artificial intelligence (AI) tools help firms analyze transaction data and identify red flags in real-time.

If a customer suddenly begins making large international wire transfers to high-risk jurisdictions, engages in high-frequency trading with no clear economic purpose, or exhibits suspicious financial behavior, the institution may need to file a Suspicious Activity Report (SAR) and conduct further investigation.

Ongoing monitoring ensures that financial firms can detect money laundering schemes as they develop rather than after illegal activities have already occurred.

INSIDER TRADING AND ETHICAL CONSIDERATIONS

Insider trading is a serious offense in financial markets, involving the buying or selling of securities based on non-public, material information. This practice gives an unfair advantage to those with privileged access to confidential corporate data, undermining market integrity and investor trust. Insider trading is illegal in most jurisdictions and is closely monitored by regulators such as the Securities and Exchange Commission (SEC) in the United States, the Financial Conduct Authority (FCA) in the United Kingdom, and other international financial watchdogs.

Ethical considerations in financial markets extend beyond legality. Even when insider trading does not technically violate laws, it may still breach ethical standards and harm investor confidence. Ethical financial behavior involves fairness, transparency, and accountability, ensuring that all market participants operate on a level playing field.

Insider trading occurs when individuals with access to non-public, material information about a company buy or sell securities before that information becomes publicly available. This gives them an unfair advantage over other investors who do not have the same knowledge.

Material information is any data that could impact a company's stock price if disclosed. This includes earnings reports, mergers and acquisitions, leadership changes, regulatory investigations, or significant business developments. Non-public information is confidential and not yet available to the general public through financial filings, press releases, or official corporate disclosures.

For example, if a corporate executive learns that their company is about to be acquired at a premium price and buys shares before the acquisition is announced, this is considered insider trading. Similarly, if an employee knows that a company is about to release poor financial results and sells their shares in advance, they are engaging in illegal activity.

Insider trading laws are designed to prevent market manipulation and ensure that all investors have equal access to information before making trading decisions. Regulators impose strict penalties on individuals and organizations found guilty of engaging in this practice.

Types of Insider Trading

Insider trading can be legal or illegal, depending on the circumstances.

1. Legal Insider Trading

Not all trading by insiders is illegal. Corporate executives, directors, and employees are allowed to buy and sell shares of their company, provided they comply with regulatory requirements. Legal insider trading occurs when:

- The insider reports their trades to the SEC and follows disclosure guidelines.
- The trade is made during approved trading windows, not immediately before major corporate announcements.
- The insider does not act on non-public material information.

Corporate insiders must file Form 4 with the SEC to disclose their transactions, ensuring that investors can track insider buying and selling activity. Some executives use Rule 10b5-1 trading plans, which allow them to pre-schedule stock trades to avoid the appearance of improper activity.

2. Illegal Insider Trading

Illegal insider trading occurs when an individual trades securities based on confidential information not available to the public. This includes not only company executives but also employees, consultants, lawyers, auditors, investment bankers, and even friends or family members who receive inside information.

Illegal insider trading can take several forms:

- Tipping – When an insider provides non-public information to someone else (such as a friend, relative, or hedge fund manager) who then trades based on that tip. Both the tipper and tippee can be held legally responsible.
- Front-running – When a broker or trader buys or sells securities based on confidential client information before executing a large order that will impact the stock price.
- Misappropriation of information – When someone outside the company (such as an attorney or investment advisor) misuses privileged information obtained in a professional capacity for personal gain.

Regulators actively monitor suspicious trading activity and impose severe penalties, including fines, disgorgement of profits, and even imprisonment for those caught engaging in illegal insider trading.

Ethical Considerations in Insider Trading

Beyond legal implications, insider trading raises significant ethical concerns related to fairness, transparency, and investor confidence. Ethical financial practices require that all market participants operate on equal footing, without privileged access to information.

When individuals engage in insider trading, they undermine trust in the integrity of financial markets. Investors expect that stock prices reflect publicly available information and that they have an equal opportunity to make informed decisions. When some traders gain an unfair advantage through confidential knowledge, it erodes confidence in the fairness of the system.

Ethical investing principles emphasize honesty, accountability, and respect for market rules. Corporate executives and financial professionals have a fiduciary duty to act in the best interests of shareholders, avoiding conflicts of interest and improper use of inside information.

Financial institutions and corporations establish strict internal policies to prevent insider trading, requiring employees to adhere to ethical trading practices. Compliance programs often include mandatory training, trading restrictions during blackout periods, and pre-clearance requirements for personal transactions.

PART 3

PRACTICE AND APPLICATION

CHAPTER 10

PRACTICE QUESTIONS AND EXAM STRATEGIES

SAMPLE QUESTIONS AND EXPLANATIONS

The Series 7 exam is designed to test a candidate's knowledge of securities markets, trading strategies, investment products, and regulatory compliance. The exam consists of 125 multiple-choice questions, and candidates must be able to analyze scenarios, apply industry rules, and demonstrate critical thinking skills.

Practicing with realistic sample questions is essential for understanding the exam structure, question types, and logic behind correct answers. Below are several sample Series 7-style questions along with detailed explanations to reinforce key concepts.

Question 1: Equity Securities

An investor purchases **200 shares of common stock** in XYZ Corporation at **$40 per share**. Five months later, XYZ Corporation announces a **2-for-1 stock split**. Following the stock split, what is the new price per share and how many shares does the investor now own?

A) New price: $20, New shares: 400
B) New price: $40, New shares: 400
C) New price: $80, New shares: 100
D) New price: $20, New shares: 200

Explanation:
Stock splits are used by companies to adjust share prices and increase liquidity in the market. A 2-for-1 stock split means that for every one share owned, investors receive two shares.

To calculate the new share count:
To calculate the new stock price:

After the split, the investor now owns 400 shares at $20 per share, maintaining the total investment value of $8,000.

Correct answer: **A) New price: $20, New shares: 400**

This question tests stock split calculations, a frequent topic in equity securities and corporate actions.

Question 2: Bonds and Interest Rates
A bond is currently trading at 102 in the secondary market. What does this mean?

A) The bond is trading at a discount.
B) The bond is trading at a premium.
C) The bond is trading at par value.
D) The bond is trading below its coupon rate.

Explanation:
Bonds are priced as a percentage of their face value, which is usually $1,000 per bond.

- If a bond trades above 100 (par value), it is trading at a premium.
- If a bond trades below 100, it is trading at a discount.
- A bond trading at exactly 100 is at par value.

A price of 102 means the bond is trading at 102% of its face value, or $1,020 per bond, indicating it is being sold at a premium.

Correct answer: **B) The bond is trading at a premium.**

This question reinforces bond pricing and market value concepts, crucial for fixed-income securities.

Question 3: Options Trading

An investor writes an ABC November 50 put option for $3 per contract. What is the investor's maximum potential loss on this trade?

A) $3 per contract
B) $47 per contract
C) $5,000 per contract
D) $4,700 per contract

Explanation:
When an investor writes (sells) a put option, they are obligated to buy the underlying stock at the strike price if the option is exercised.

The maximum loss occurs if the stock price falls to $0, meaning the investor must buy the stock at $50 per share while it becomes worthless.

Correct answer: **D) $4,700 per contract**

This question evaluates understanding of option risk, obligation for put sellers, and maximum loss scenarios.

Question 4: Mutual Fund Regulations

Which of the following statements about mutual fund sales charges is **true**?

A) Class A shares have the highest ongoing fees but no upfront charge.
B) Class B shares have no upfront sales charge but higher ongoing fees.
C) Class C shares convert to Class A shares over time, reducing expenses.
D) Class B shares have lower expense ratios than Class A shares.

Explanation:
Mutual funds have different share classes, each with unique fee structures.

- Class A shares have an upfront sales charge (load) but lower annual expenses.
- Class B shares do not have an upfront charge but have higher annual fees and a contingent deferred sales charge (CDSC) if sold within a certain period.

- Class C shares have higher ongoing fees and do not convert into Class A shares.
- Class B shares generally have higher expense ratios than Class A shares due to deferred sales charges.

Correct answer: **B) Class B shares have no upfront sales charge but higher ongoing fees.**

This question ensures candidates understand mutual fund share classes and sales charge structures.

Question 5: Margin Trading Rules

A customer opens a margin account and purchases $40,000 worth of securities. According to Regulation T, what is the minimum initial deposit required?

A) $2,000
B) $10,000
C) $20,000
D) $40,000

Explanation:

Regulation T requires an initial deposit of at least 50% of the purchase price for margin accounts.

Additionally, the minimum margin requirement for new accounts is $2,000, but since the required margin is higher ($20,000), that rule does not apply here. **

Correct answer: **C) $20,000**

This question reinforces Regulation T and initial margin requirements for leverage trading.

Why Practicing Sample Questions Is Important

Practicing Series 7-style questions helps develop:

1. Familiarity with exam structure – Understanding how questions are phrased reduces exam-day surprises.
2. Ability to analyze scenarios – Many questions require applying knowledge to real-world trading situations.
3. Time management – Regular practice improves efficiency in handling complex calculations and regulatory-based questions.
4. Confidence – The more candidates practice, the more they understand patterns, logic, and reasoning behind correct answers.

TIME MANAGEMENT ON THE EXAM

The Series 7 exam is a challenging, time-intensive test, requiring candidates to answer 125 multiple-choice questions within 225 minutes (3 hours and 45 minutes). This means candidates have an average of 1.8 minutes per question. Effective time management strategies are crucial to ensure all questions are answered within the allotted time while maintaining accuracy. Poor time management can lead to rushing, misreading questions, careless mistakes, and running out of time before completing the test.

Understanding the Exam Structure for Better Time Allocation

The Series 7 exam consists of four sections covering different topics. Some sections may have more straightforward factual questions, while others may require complex calculations or regulatory interpretation. Candidates should be aware of which topics typically take longer so they can budget time accordingly.

The general breakdown of the Series 7 exam content is as follows:

- Equity and Debt Securities (35-40% of the exam) – Involves understanding stocks, bonds, dividends, and corporate actions. Some questions require calculations related to yield, pricing, and total return, which can take more time.
- Options Trading and Strategies (15-20%) – Includes complex option pricing, breakeven calculations, and multi-leg strategies. These are often among the most time-consuming questions.
- Mutual Funds, Annuities, and Retirement Plans (15-20%) – Mostly concept-based, but some questions require analysis of fund fees and tax implications.
- Regulatory and Ethical Considerations (20-25%) – Primarily conceptual but requires careful reading to interpret regulatory scenarios correctly.

Candidates should allocate more time for sections that require calculations and in-depth analysis, while answering straightforward factual questions quickly to save time for the more challenging ones.

Time Allocation Strategies for the Series 7 Exam

To maximize efficiency during the exam, candidates should divide their time strategically and ensure they stay on track throughout the test. Below is a time management plan based on a 225-minute exam duration:

1. Budgeting Time Per Question

Since candidates have **1.8 minutes per question**, the following guidelines help maintain an efficient pace:

- Quick, definition-based questions (30-40% of the exam) – Spend 30-60 seconds per question. These include direct regulatory rules, concept-based questions, and basic trading principles.
- Scenario-based questions (30-40%) – Spend 1-2 minutes on questions requiring reasoning and application of industry rules. These often describe a client's financial profile and require choosing the best course of action.
- Calculation-heavy questions (20-30%) – Spend no more than 2-3 minutes per question. If a question is taking too long, mark it for review and move forward to prevent losing valuable time.

Candidates should aim to complete the first 50 questions within 90 minutes, allowing ample time for remaining sections and review.

2. Answering Questions Efficiently

Start with the easiest questions first. If a question can be answered instantly, complete it and move on. This builds momentum and ensures that maximum questions are completed before tackling difficult ones.

If a question seems unclear or overly complex, skip it and return later. Spending too much time on one question can create unnecessary time pressure for the rest of the exam.

Flagging questions for later review is a valuable strategy. If a question requires deeper thought, selecting the best initial guess and marking it for review allows candidates to return with a fresh perspective if time remains.

3. Managing Difficult Questions

Difficult questions often include:

- Options pricing and multi-leg strategies – These may require multiple calculations, so use educated guessing if necessary and come back later if time permits.
- Bond yield and pricing calculations – If a problem takes longer than two minutes, consider moving on and revisiting it at the end.
- Regulatory interpretation questions – These often involve long paragraphs and case-based scenarios. Carefully identify key terms and eliminate incorrect answers quickly.

The goal is to **complete as many questions as possible efficiently**, ensuring that no easy points are missed while working through complex problems.

Tips to Stay on Track During the Exam

1. Using the Process of Elimination

Many Series 7 questions include distracting answer choices designed to test precision. Candidates should:

- Immediately eliminate incorrect answers to narrow choices.
- Identify extreme statements – If an answer seems too absolute, it is likely incorrect.
- Look for keywords in the question that match with possible correct responses.

2. Avoiding Overthinking

It is easy to overanalyze a question and waste time reconsidering answers. Candidates should trust their preparation and avoid second-guessing answers unless they clearly misread the question.

- If an answer seems correct, go with it and move forward.
- Do not change answers unless absolutely necessary – Statistics show that first instincts are often correct.

3. Sticking to a Time Check System

To stay on pace, candidates should check their progress at key points in the exam:

- After 60 minutes – Should have completed at least 30-40 questions.
- After 120 minutes – Should be past the halfway mark (65-70 questions).
- With 30 minutes remaining – Should have only flagged or difficult questions left.

This ensures that no section is rushed at the end, allowing time for thoughtful review of uncertain answers.

4. Managing Test Anxiety and Mental Fatigue

Since the Series 7 exam lasts nearly four hours, mental fatigue can set in. Candidates should:

- Take brief mental breaks – Closing eyes for 10-15 seconds between difficult questions helps refocus.
- Practice deep breathing techniques if anxiety rises.
- Avoid fixating on past mistakes – If a question was difficult, move on rather than letting it affect the next one.

Candidates who feel overwhelmed should take a short pause (without losing too much time) to reset their focus.

Final 10-Minute Review Strategy

The last 10 minutes of the exam should be used strategically:

- Revisit flagged questions – Prioritize those that require additional thought.
- Check for skipped questions – Ensure no question was left blank, as unanswered questions are marked incorrect.
- Verify calculation-based responses – Quickly confirm any bond yield, option breakeven, or total return calculations.

By managing time effectively throughout the test, candidates can maximize accuracy, complete all questions, and reduce test-day stress.

HANDLING TRICKY OR CONFUSING QUESTIONS

The Series 7 exam contains a mix of straightforward, conceptual, and complex scenario-based questions that require critical thinking. While some questions can be answered quickly, others may be tricky due to ambiguous wording, multiple correct-looking choices, or calculations with misleading details. Candidates must develop strategies to identify traps, break down complex scenarios, and eliminate incorrect answers efficiently.

Tricky questions are designed to test candidates' attention to detail, regulatory knowledge, and ability to apply industry rules under different circumstances. To handle such questions effectively, candidates should use structured problem-solving methods, logical reasoning, and a systematic approach to answering.

Identifying Tricky Questions on the Series 7 Exam

Some questions are deliberately written to confuse test-takers by including excess details, closely related answer choices, or regulatory exceptions. Common types of tricky questions include:

- Scenario-Based Questions with Extra Information – These questions may include irrelevant details to distract candidates from the core issue.
- Double-Negative or Reverse-Worded Questions – Phrased in a way that requires extra attention to avoid misinterpretation.
- Regulatory Questions with Exceptions – Test whether candidates remember specific rule exemptions or special conditions.
- Computation-Based Questions with Decoy Answers – Involve calculations where incorrect answers resemble common calculation mistakes.
- "Most Likely" or "Best Answer" Questions – Where multiple answers seem correct, but only one is the best industry practice.

Recognizing these question types early helps candidates approach them methodically rather than rushing and falling into traps.

Techniques for Answering Tricky Questions Effectively

1. Read the Question Carefully Before Looking at Answer Choices

A common mistake candidates make is glancing at answer choices too soon, which can create confusion. Instead, follow these steps:

1. Read the question fully before checking the answers. Ensure you understand the core concept being tested.
2. Identify key terms. Look for important details such as transaction types, client objectives, regulatory constraints, or numerical values.
3. Determine what the question is asking. Many questions contain excess information that doesn't impact the answer. Ignore distractions and focus only on what is relevant.

For example, a question might present a client's full financial profile before asking about a suitable investment. Instead of analyzing every detail, pinpoint the key risk factors, time horizon, and investor goals.

2. Be Careful with Double-Negative or Reverse-Worded Questions

Some tricky questions use **negative phrasing**, which can mislead test-takers into selecting the wrong answer. Examples include:

- "Which of the following is NOT required for…"
- "All of the following are true EXCEPT…"
- "Which of the following is LEAST likely to…"

The best way to handle such questions is to rewrite them in a straightforward manner before answering.

Example Question:

"Which of the following statements is NOT correct regarding mutual fund share classes?"

A) Class A shares typically have a front-end sales charge.
B) Class B shares convert to Class A shares over time.
C) Class C shares generally have lower annual expenses than Class A shares.
D) Class B shares have contingent deferred sales charges if sold early.

Correct Answer: **C) Class C shares generally have lower annual expenses than Class A shares.**

Why? The question asks for the incorrect statement, so instead of searching for the right answer, identify the false statement. Class C shares tend to have higher ongoing expenses than Class A shares, making answer C incorrect.

When encountering a negative question, take a moment to rephrase it as a positive question to avoid confusion.

3. Eliminate Obviously Wrong Answer Choices First

For difficult questions, eliminating **incorrect choices first** improves the odds of selecting the correct answer. Use a **systematic approach**:

1. Immediately rule out incorrect or extreme statements.
2. Compare the remaining choices logically.
3. Use test-taking intuition—avoid answers that sound overly complicated or contradict key concepts.

Example Question:
A client wants a low-risk, tax-efficient investment with stable income. Which of the following would be the most suitable recommendation?

A) High-yield corporate bonds
B) Tax-exempt municipal bonds
C) Growth-oriented mutual funds
D) Speculative stock options

Step-by-step elimination:

- High-yield corporate bonds carry higher risk (eliminate).
- Growth-oriented mutual funds focus on capital appreciation, not income (eliminate).
- Speculative stock options involve high volatility (eliminate).
- Tax-exempt municipal bonds provide stable, low-risk income, making B the best choice.

Using elimination helps narrow down answer choices quickly, reducing second-guessing.

4. Watch Out for Distracting Answer Choices That Sound Correct

Many tricky questions include answer choices that seem partially correct but are not the best answer. To handle this:

- Identify the most accurate and complete answer.
- Avoid answers that make broad, absolute claims (e.g., "Always" or "Never").
- Be cautious of answers that use uncommon terminology.

Example Question:
Under **FINRA rules**, what is the maximum annual gift value that a registered representative can give to a client without violating industry regulations?

A) $500
B) $250
C) $100
D) Unlimited if disclosed

The most common mistake here is choosing **$250 or $500**, but FINRA **strictly limits gifts to $100 per year per recipient**.

Correct Answer: **C) $100**

Tricky questions often **include incorrect numerical values that seem reasonable**, so remembering key regulations is essential.

5. Use Logical Reasoning on Questions with Multiple "Correct" Answers
Some questions have multiple correct-looking choices, requiring candidates to select the best possible answer based on industry standards.

Example Question:
A client with a **moderate risk tolerance and a long-term investment horizon** wants a diversified portfolio. Which is the **most suitable** investment recommendation?

A) 100% high-yield bonds
B) 100% large-cap value stocks

C) A balanced mutual fund
D) Short-term money market funds

While high-yield bonds (A) and large-cap stocks (B) offer growth, they lack diversification. Short-term money markets (D) focus on capital preservation but do not align with long-term growth needs. The best answer is C, a balanced mutual fund, as it provides diversification, risk control, and long-term growth potential.

When multiple answers seem correct, ask:

- Which answer meets the client's needs while balancing risk?
- Which choice aligns with FINRA's suitability rules?
- Which is the most complete, industry-standard response?

Final Tips for Handling Tricky Questions

1. Don't Rush. Take the time to fully understand what's being asked before selecting an answer.
2. Skip and Return Later. If unsure, mark the question and revisit it after completing easier ones.
3. Break Down Complex Scenarios. If a question is long, identify key financial details and ignore distractions.
4. Trust Your Preparation. If two answers seem similar, go with your first instinct unless you recognize a clear mistake.
5. Stay Calm. Even if a question is confusing, avoid panic. Use logic and elimination to make the best decision.

By following these strategies, candidates can approach tricky Series 7 questions with confidence, improve accuracy, and maximize their chances of passing the exam.

CHAPTER 11

SIMULATED PRACTICE EXAMS

Below is a simulated full-length Series 7 practice test designed to reflect the format, structure, and difficulty level of the actual exam. This test consists of 14 out of 125 multiple-choice questions, covering all major topics, including equity and debt securities, options, mutual funds, retirement accounts, regulatory rules, and trading strategies.

Candidates should complete the test under timed conditions (225 minutes) to simulate real exam conditions.

FULL-LENGTH PRACTICE TEST (125 QUESTIONS)

Equity Securities (Common and Preferred Stock, Corporate Actions) – 15 Questions

1. A stockholder who owns common shares in a company has which of the following rights?

A) Guaranteed dividend payments

B) Right to vote on corporate policies

C) First claim on company assets during liquidation

D) Right to determine executive salaries

2. When a company declares a 3-for-2 stock split, how many shares will an investor own if they originally had 200 shares?
A) 300
B) 133
C) 400
D) 250

3. What is the primary reason a company may issue preferred stock?
A) To increase debt liabilities
B) To offer shareholders voting rights
C) To raise capital without diluting common stock voting power
D) To guarantee long-term capital gains

Debt Securities (Bonds, Yields, Interest Rates) – 15 Questions

4. A 10-year corporate bond with a 6% coupon is currently trading at 90 in the secondary market. What is the bond trading at?
A) Discount
B) Par value
C) Premium
D) Callable price

5. If interest rates **fall**, which type of bond will experience the **greatest price increase**?

A) A 5-year bond with a 3% coupon
B) A 10-year zero-coupon bond
C) A 20-year bond with a 6% coupon
D) A Treasury Bill

Options (Calls, Puts, Strategies, Pricing) – 15 Questions

6. A customer buys an ABC **June 40 Call at $4**. What is the breakeven price?
A) $36
B) $40
C) $44
D) $46

7. If an investor wants to **generate income on a stock position, they already own**, which of the following strategies is most appropriate?
A) Buying a protective put
B) Selling a covered call
C) Writing an uncovered call
D) Buying a straddle

Mutual Funds and Investment Companies – 15 Questions

8. Which type of mutual fund class has an **upfront sales charge** but lower annual expenses?
A) Class A shares
B) Class B shares
C) Class C shares
D) No-load funds

9. What is the primary benefit of investing in a mutual fund rather than individual stocks?
A) Higher risk potential
B) Greater diversification
C) Unlimited short selling opportunities

D) Tax-free capital gains

Margin Trading and Trading Accounts – 15 Questions

10. According to **Regulation T**, what is the **initial margin requirement** when purchasing securities on margin?
A) 25%
B) 50%
C) 75%
D) 100%

11. If a margin account has a **maintenance margin requirement of 25%**, what happens when an investor's equity falls below this level?
A) A margin call is issued
B) The broker loans additional funds
C) The investor is required to close their account
D) No action is necessary

Retirement Accounts and Tax-Advantaged Investments – 10 Questions

12. Which of the following statements about **Roth IRAs** is **true**?
A) Contributions are tax-deductible
B) Withdrawals in retirement are tax-free
C) There are required minimum distributions (RMDs)
D) Earnings are taxed as ordinary income upon withdrawal

Regulations and Compliance – 10 Questions

13. Under **FINRA Rule 3220**, what is the maximum gift a registered representative can give to a client per year?

A) $50

B) $100

C) $250

D) Unlimited if disclosed

14. The **Securities Exchange Act of 1934** primarily regulates which of the following?

A) Initial Public Offerings (IPOs)

B) Trading of securities in secondary markets

C) Registration of new mutual funds

D) Taxation of capital gains

ANSWER KEY AND EXPLANATIONS

After completing the practice test, use the answer key below to check responses and review explanations for each question.

Equity Securities Answer Explanations

1. **B) Right to vote on corporate policies** – Common stockholders vote on corporate decisions, but dividends are not guaranteed.
2. **A) 300** – A 3-for-2 stock split means an investor receives 3 shares for every 2 owned.
3. **C) To raise capital without diluting common stock voting power** – Preferred stock allows a company to raise funds without affecting common shareholder votes.

Debt Securities Answer Explanations

4. **A) Discount** – A bond trading below par (100) is at a discount.
5. **B) A 10-year zero-coupon bond** – Longer-term and zero-coupon bonds are most sensitive to interest rate changes.

Options Answer Explanations

6. **C) $44** – Breakeven for a call option = Strike Price + Premium Paid ($40 + $4).
7. **B) Selling a covered call** – Generates income by selling call options on stocks already owned.

Mutual Funds Answer Explanations

8. **A) Class A shares** – Class A shares have a front-end sales charge but lower annual expenses.
9. **B) Greater diversification** – Mutual funds reduce risk by spreading investments across different assets.

Margin Trading Answer Explanations

10. **B) 50%** – Regulation T requires an initial margin deposit of 50% of the purchase price.
11. **A) A margin call is issued** – If equity falls below maintenance margin, a margin call requires the investor to deposit more funds.

Retirement Accounts Answer Explanations

12. **B) Withdrawals in retirement are tax-free** – Roth IRA contributions are made with after-tax dollars, making retirement withdrawals tax-free.

Regulations and Compliance Answer Explanations

13. **B) $100** – FINRA's annual gift limit per client is $100.
14. **B) Trading of securities in secondary markets** – The **Securities Exchange Act of 1934** governs secondary market trading and broker-dealer regulations.

CONCLUSION

The Series 7 exam is a challenging yet rewarding milestone for anyone pursuing a career as a securities representative. Success requires strong preparation, effective test-taking strategies, and a thorough understanding of financial products, regulations, and market operations. With dedication, practice, and proper time management, candidates can maximize their chances of passing on the first attempt.

Final Tips and Reminders

As the exam day approaches, candidates should focus on consolidating knowledge and maintaining confidence. Here are some essential last-minute tips:

- Review high-priority topics – Ensure mastery of key concepts such as equities, bonds, options, regulatory compliance, and margin trading.
- Memorize formulas and rules – Important calculations (e.g., option breakeven prices, bond yields, margin requirements) should be second nature.
- Use practice exams effectively – Focus on questions you previously got wrong and understand why the correct answers are right.
- Avoid cramming – Instead of trying to learn new material at the last minute, review summary notes and key takeaways.

- Stay confident – Trust your preparation and approach the test with a calm and focused mindset.

Day-Before-Exam Checklist

The night before the Series 7 exam, candidates should ensure they are fully prepared by following this checklist:

✓ Confirm exam logistics – Double-check the exam date, time, location, and identification requirements. Arrive at least 30 minutes early to allow time for check-in.
✓ Prepare required items – Bring valid identification (government-issued ID), a calculator (if permitted), and exam admission confirmation.
✓ Get a good night's sleep – Avoid staying up late reviewing materials. A well-rested mind performs significantly better under exam conditions.
✓ Eat a balanced meal – Have a nutritious breakfast to maintain focus and energy throughout the exam. Avoid excessive caffeine to prevent jitters.
✓ Stay relaxed – Engage in light physical activity or deep breathing exercises to reduce anxiety. Visualize a successful exam outcome.

What to Expect After Passing the Exam

Once a candidate successfully passes the Series 7 exam, they officially become a General Securities Representative, allowing them to trade stocks, bonds, mutual funds, options, and other securities. However, additional steps may still be required:

- Sponsoring firm registration – The candidate's brokerage firm must officially register them with FINRA before they can begin selling securities.
- Continuing education requirements – Securities professionals must complete ongoing training and compliance courses to maintain their license.
- Additional licensing (if required) – Some firms may require representatives to obtain other FINRA licenses, such as the Series 63 (State Law Exam) or Series 66 (Investment Advisor Exam).

Next Steps in Your Career

After passing the Series 7 exam, professionals can pursue several career paths, including:

- Becoming a stockbroker or financial advisor – Work with clients to develop investment strategies, trade securities, and manage portfolios.
- Exploring specialized roles – Gain expertise in options trading, wealth management, or investment banking.
- Advancing through additional certifications – Consider obtaining the Series 24 (Principal Exam) for supervisory roles or the Chartered Financial Analyst (CFA) designation for in-depth investment research.

Passing the Series 7 is just the beginning of a rewarding financial career. With dedication, ethical conduct, and continued learning, successful candidates can build strong client relationships, expand their expertise, and achieve long-term success in the securities industry.

www.ingramcontent.com/pod-product-compliance
Lightning Source LLC
LaVergne TN
LVHW090402210926
848480LV00002B/428